WARRIOR LEADERSHIP

*Steps to Success for
Leaders on the Ground*

JB Spisso

Library of Congress Control Number: 2019909491

ISBN: 978-1-7332758-0-4

First Printing: July 2019

Published by: JBS Leadership Consultants, LLC
Henderson, NV

Back Cover Photo: Hugh Roberts - @hughportraits

DEDICATION

For my children,

Mara, Marco, and Abra Dian

Wonderful warriors who inspire each and every day.

FOREWORD

I have known JB Spisso well for many years. This man is the consummate motivator and team builder. He is a true leader. Some of his unique talent he was born with. The rest he learned along the way in the school of hard knocks, most notably in the trenches in one of the most elite units in America's arsenal, the 75th Ranger Regiment.

JB Spisso has a passion for passing on those lessons. He is at his best when surrounded by a group of young men and women, who, after exposure to JB are transformed into pursuing personal goals of being the best leader or team member they can be. While at West Point, I have stared into the eyes of his charges at the end of his training and have witnessed this transformation. They emerged more confident, more focused, and more driven to succeed. What before had been self-absorbed youths bent on the pursuit of personal comfort, morphed into a robust, team-centered, warrior legion, ready to take charge and take the hill.

I watched JB take over a moribund National Guard organization as a Senior Sergeant. In very little time, he turned the Officer Candidate School at Camp Smith, New York into an environment that encouraged dynamic, impressive motivation and produced top-quality young officers eager and ready to lead, many of whom went on to distinguish themselves in action overseas.

His work with the hockey teams from prep schools and from the NHL has yielded similar success. Young, self-centered men transformed into people who were team-focused and ignored personal fatigue and injuries to rally themselves and those around them to do their best.

Like everyone else, JB Spisso's life has not been without his dark periods. On a rare few, his success and star quality have had a negative effect, producing jealously in fellow workers and those who stand outside the arena; those who cannot do what he does; those who wallow in self-pity and lethargy. However, that too is part of the story. We will all get knocked down – it's whether we get back on our feet and continue the attack that is the mark of real character. JB has that mark.

Warrior Leadership captures the essence of JB's leadership philosophy in a conversational tone that will make readers feel like they are sitting across from the man at his kitchen table. This book is a must for those seeking to improve themselves and bring their team to its peak performance.

Hank Keirsey

Hank Keirsey
Lieutenant Colonel (Retired)
U.S. Army

CONTENTS

MY LEADERSHIP JOURNEY

"The final test of a leader is that he leaves behind in others the conviction and will to carry on."
~ Walter Lippmann

I spent just over 26 years in the U.S. Army serving with some of the finest men and women our Nation has to offer. This is where I forged my foundation to do what I do best, and that's lead with a passion. My goal is simple, to help transform individuals into leaders and the remarkable people and assignments throughout my career have solidified that. Marvelous assignments in Special Operations with the 75th Ranger Regiment, as a Drill Instructor and cadre at both the United States Military Academy at West Point and Officers Candidate School. It was truly my honor for the responsibility to educate and inspire Soldiers and Cadets in the essence of war-fighting and the Profession of Arms in order to develop the proper values, leadership skills, military skills, character, and warrior ethos to effectively lead America's Soldiers. I was able to do this at all levels, finally retiring at the rank of Sergeant Major, the highest and most respected Non-Commissioned Officer rank in the U.S. military. Whatever I taught, I learned ten-fold in return, and sincere thanks will never be enough.

Many years ago, I was delivering a leadership seminar to a group of business professionals, and during the session, I told a few stories about my career that generally cause people to laugh. A funny mistake I made, or an action where poking fun at myself shows that leaders are not infallible. At the end of the session a woman and very senior member of their executive staff came up to me, and at first, I thought she was upset for a few choice words I used during the event. Instead, she introduced herself, told me what she did, and said she had spent countless hours and thousands of dollars on leadership seminars and motivational speakers throughout her life and business career. She rattled off a who's who laundry list of keynote speakers as if she had rehearsed this prior. This list included former U.S. Presidents, CEO's, as well as the most popular motivational speakers. She then pointed at my chest and said, "Do you know what you have over those people?" Politely I said, "No, Ma'am." She replied, "You're real; those other speakers tell us what we want to hear. You have a great message; don't ever change!" I said, "Thank You." She shook my hand, walked off, and after getting a few feet away, turned around, and said, "Oh, and write a book, you have a lot to offer!"

So here I am, many years later but never forgetting the message she gave me. It took me a while to have the personal courage to write down my thoughts on leadership. All leaders feel like they have something to offer, but was there something in my story that could trigger something for another leader? After years of evaluating, and some friendly reminders from people whom I trust, I finally put my thoughts on paper. Though I'm hoping this book is read by leaders at all levels as there are parts applicable to everyone from the CEO/General Officer to the newly appointed and up and coming manager, this book is for leaders on the ground. The man or woman who is in charge of two people, or two hundred; someone who is out there every day getting it done and trying to do it the right way.

Great leaders are not only able to develop detailed plans and objectives for goals, projects, and missions, but also able to lead their people through practices that offer supervision, refinement, and inspection. Finally, being able to execute stated objectives accurately and on time will be your best architect for credibility. This book isn't about having all the right answers; frankly, you won't always have the correct answers. It's about finding solutions that result in attaining goals. Execution is the key to success, and if you have the bulk of the project planned and completed, get out there and get it done, on time!

There are plenty of books about jumping to the top; this book isn't one of them. Everything is this book is going to lead back to three things:

- Hard work
- Staying positive
- Leadership is a learning process

*"The 80% plan executed on time is better than the
100% plan executed late!"*
~ CDR (Ret) Chris "Spanky" Frasse, USN, DEVGRU

I am gratified by my military service, each day serving our Country proudly and honorably. I was fortunate to have served with the finest men and women our Country has to offer. Though I did a lot of great things in the military, I have never considered myself a hero; instead, I was extremely fortunate to have served amongst Heroes.

Finally, this book is about my leadership and life experiences, and no two people see things the same way. Everything in this book is how I remember it, and if there are any inaccuracies, they are my responsibility. Nothing in this book is classified. I hope you enjoy it! Hooah!

JB Spisso

WARRIORS LEARN FROM WARRIORS

As a modern-day leadership and culture development expert, and performance consultant, I often speak about the three key attributes that define the best and what I challenge everyone to be. These are being a *warrior, winner, and leader.* Though only three simple words, they are very complex. At any time, you can exemplify one or more of these attributes. For example, you can't be a winner if you're not gracious, or you are a sore loser. Winning is the action, but a "winner" is what defines the attribute.

I often ask clients what their definition of a warrior is. What do they believe embodies a warrior and more importantly, can they give me an example of one? A warrior is not only a Spartan jumping off the rock impaling the enemy with his spear. Being a warrior is much more than the physical attributes (though they do play a part). Being a warrior is working hard to be the best at whatever you do and doing it with honor, personal courage, and character. Mother Theresa doesn't look like a Spartan fighter, but is she a warrior? Of course, she is! The leadership point here is that your inner-warrior attributes teach the people around you to be warriors.

One of the greatest Warriors in my lifetime was Patricia G. Spisso. She was not only a brilliant educator and champion for human rights, but also the greatest mother any family could ever hope to have. Warriors learn from warriors, and we learned from the best!

She set the bar high for my warrior traits and ethos and did so with a kind heart, gentle touch, and a brilliant mind that taught my family toughness, humility, and passion.

Toughness is a trait often mistaken for someone with a rough exterior and attitude to match. Being tough has nothing to do with being cold, callous, mean or aggressive. Toughness is the ability to do the right things, despite the "crowd's opinion" or personal consequences. Today we have many people displaying what they think is toughness over social media when, in reality, they are just bullying or being part of the "mob."

My mother had the look of an Italian movie star and the toughness of a Spartan Queen. She stood for Women's Rights in the most unpopular times and squared off against some of the most chauvinistic and egomaniac men that Western Pennsylvania had to offer. Her battle armor was her spirit, her mind, and knowing she was making life better for others. She always wore her "shoes of peace" yet had the gladiator sword and shield ready in case it was needed. As a brilliant educator (41 years), she worked tirelessly to help the children of the wealthy, middle-class, and poor receive an education. She showed families from all walks of life how to succeed, how to move forward, and especially how to do it with the humility necessary.

She challenged my two older sisters and me to leave a "footprint" in life. Mom always said if we did it the right way with honor, personal courage, and integrity that others would use our path for their success. She never let herself be bogged down with negativity or negative people, and taught us to do the same. If you wanted my mother's help, you better show up positive and ready to work; the "oh poor me" attitude was never accepted.

My mother didn't come from money nor married into it; she and my father raised three successful children on a middle-class budget and inspired all of us to follow our dreams and leave that "impression." We all have that work ethic, and though we might have a few more material things than our parents did; the values we have learned are the foundation. My mother and father were married over 53 years, and they were examples of how to live a healthy, blissful marriage.

Warriors learn from Warriors. Teach, coach, mentor, train, inspire, be passionate, and motivate; these are what I do best, but only because I learned from the best.

Rest in Peace Mother; you will never be forgotten!

The Take-Away

Warriors come in all shapes and sizes; the primary point of being a warrior is be the best at what you do. Leave a footprint in life! Teach, coach, and mentor. Find a warrior in your life and learn from them.

FINDING YOUR LEADERSHIP STYLE

Throughout my 26-year military career, I was often asked to define my leadership style and to give suggestions on which method I think young leaders should adopt. First off, let's review some common leadership styles and ones that I have seen throughout my experiences.

Micromanager	Team Player
Screamer	Cheerleader
Narcissist (egomaniac)	Ambassador/Diplomat
Warrior	Risk-averse
Quiet Professional	Communicator

This is not an exhaustive list as I'm sure there are hundreds of leadership books outlining specifics. Some of these leadership styles I go into in greater detail in other parts of this book. The critical point is to mold your leadership style by what works for you as a leader and a human being. It must be positive, moral, ethical, and your leadership style should require YOU to be the ultimate team player. You need to be authentic. Your style should be free from entitlement and should treat people with respect. Yes, sometimes as leaders we must be very "pointed and direct" in our method; however, you can be professional and non-abrasive in this approach, and this should be your daily goal.

When I was a young 18-year-old Ranger in 2nd Ranger Battalion, I was fortunate to have a great Squad Leader by the name of Staff Sergeant (SSG) Hugh Roberts. SSG Roberts was very well respected; from the first day in his squad, he encouraged all of us to find our own identity in how we would lead. Some felt the need to be the constant hard case, while others wanted to be everyone's buddy. While some squad leaders wanted carbon copies of themselves, SSG Roberts wanted bright individuals with an independent thought process that put the mission and their mates at the forefront. The most valuable lesson I learned from SSG Roberts was that you could have more than one leadership style as circumstances dictated, but it was important to be consistent.

SSG Roberts was a physical fitness machine and could run us all into the ground. He knew when to yell, and when to pat us on the back, and we all knew the lines not to cross. If you did something that embarrassed the squad, you were going to pay the price. Furthermore, if you excelled during military training, he openly recognized you. He was a great teacher. He took the time to communicate to us, not only the specifics out of the manual, but also the techniques for success that aren't printed in the book. He never allowed us to take shortcuts, and he settled for nothing less than our best every day. He also respected everyone's personal values and religious beliefs.

I remember during a week-long field training exercise we had been going non-stop for over 72 hours. We finally had a few hours in the field to catch some sleep, and he told all of us to get some shut-eye while he stayed up and pulled security watching over us.

Years later, I became a Staff Sergeant, with an opportunity to pass the lessons I learned onto young Soldiers. Hugh Roberts is the calm and collected example I've always used to lead others by.

In my many years at West Point, I worked with some of the best military and civilian government leaders our Country had to offer. Cadets would prepare for graduation and look to the cadre (leaders) of West Point to find the leadership style that most aligned with them. Some cadre would say, "When you take over your platoon, make sure you go in tough; you don't get a second chance to set the tone." Something like, "You better tell your subordinates who's in charge from day one, they are not your friends." My message to young Officers as taught to me by SSG Roberts, was simply just *"be you!"*

Don't try to copy someone else, use the positive lessons of those who came before you, and make your own path. Regardless if you are taking over the best or worst team, or the best or worst department, my recommendation for your introduction should be the same; *"Hi, I'm Jim Smith, I look forward to meeting all of you and working together, and I'm damn glad to be here!"* That's it! Simple! Everyone knows your name, what you are here for, and regardless of the situation, you are excited; this will set the tone. You should never say things like; *"I'm here to fix this place,"* or *"I'm going to turn this department into something."*

Here is what every new leader needs to do to be successful:

- When taking over an organization always reiterate, "I'm glad to be here!" Under no circumstances say, "you're in charge." The people under your responsibility know this.
- Give clear direction and distance. Tell them which way to go and how far it is.
- Your people need to know what the normal operating procedures are (SOP's if you will). If they are not meeting the goals and objectives, outline how you plan to assist and lead them to meet and even exceed these requirements.
- Finally, let them know what you want to be done by when and the purpose. (The who, what, where, when, and why. You usually don't need to tell them how.)

If straightforward direction is needed, you will have to be a candid communicator. Choose the right tone and temperament. Keep in mind when a new leader comes in, everyone is gauging where the direction will go so the clearer and more concise you can be, the better it will go toward establishing the desired work ethic. People don't fear change, that's a common misconception; however, people do fear loss. So, your team will have a better understanding of the change if you clearly define what's expected.

To be a great leader, you need to be well-versed in MANY leadership styles (choose positive ones). You become more proficient at these leadership styles through *EXPERIENCE*. Remember, you are always learning.

When I retired from the Army in 2010, a well-respected Division Command Sergeant Major who knew me at previous ranks, came up to me and told me I finally had a great balance in my leadership style. He complimented me and was sincerely happy for me. I respectfully told him, "Thank you; it took me 26 years to get here!"

If you are a leader or plan on being one, hang in there, get a little better every day, and you will be OK!

The Take-Away

Develop your own leadership style.
Learning and experience go hand in hand.
Give clear and concise direction; this eliminates any misunderstanding between you (the sender) and the receiver (those under your charge).

LEAD AT ANY AGE

Many times, we are wrapped up in the age factor when it comes to making a competent leader. Yes, experience is a huge part, and I've talked about the importance of that already. However, there are times when you just have to "cowboy up" and make a decision. Learn from it, live with it, and most importantly grow from it.

Recently a business client that I life coach told me a story on how he gave one of his young brokers a project to finish. He brought the young man in on the project, and he was receiving an equal share. When it came down to the final editing before it went off to legal, the young broker just assumed his boss was going to do it. The boss said to the young broker, "Figure it out. You're talented and educated, and if you make a mistake, we will live with it." This is a lesson we all can learn from.

I joined the Army towards the end of high school because I wanted to pay for my own college instead of burdening my hard-working parents. So, I decided to sign up for something "tough" and get the college fund. The Army recruiters said all the right things and found me a "cool job" that interested me. The Army recruiter said, "Why don't you be an Army Ranger?" I replied, "What do they do?" In an eloquent tone, the recruiter calmly said, "They jump out of airplanes and blow shit up!" The rest, as they say, is history!

Coming from a small suburb outside of Pittsburgh, Pennsylvania and getting off the bus at Basic Training at Fort Benning, Georgia, was an entirely new experience for me and one that required a new level of toughness. Anyone who says they can get off the bus, see a Drill Instructor and not be even a little intimidated is lying! I was scared to death, and later in my career, I learned the other side of the fear factor as a Drill Instructor myself.

Our training lasted 13 weeks at what's known as the "Home of the Infantry" in World War II style barracks in late summer temperatures in Georgia. We had come back from our second afternoon of physical training (PT) or "smoke session" of the day, and the blistering weather was crushing us. I hear Senior Drill Sergeant Paniagua call my name, bellowing it from the second-floor window of the barracks. "Speezeeo, get up here," he called. (Drill Sergeant Paniagua couldn't pronounce my name, but that was close enough, and I wasn't correcting him!) I screeched back, "Moving Drill Sergeant!" I entered the office and stood on the mark they had painted on the floor eloquently known as the "kill zone." Paniagua looked at me and asked me how old I was to which I replied, *"18, Drill Sergeant."* He then went on to say a few things I really can't recall, but his final statement I've never forgotten. He said, "Speezeeo, you're the Platoon Leader, don't fu#k it up." I looked at him in bewilderment, not understanding what a Platoon Leader is and more importantly, what the hell was I supposed to do? He could see the puzzlement in my face, and, as the wise man he was, interjected with, "Don't worry Speezeeo, we'll help you through this now get the hell out of here!" To which I barked, "Moving Drill Sergeant!" and ran back downstairs wondering why the hell they picked me and what should I be doing?

Throughout the weeks, the Drill Instructors did as they promised and helped me forge a leadership foundation; however, they were also evident not to give me all the answers. I made many mistakes, and I paid for them in push-ups, yet while other student Platoon Leaders were changed out, I remained in my position throughout the rest of the cycle. I learned if you kept the platoon informed and kept accountability of every person, then almost everything was self-supporting. You couldn't go in to see the Drill Instructors every five minutes with a question, so I learned quickly to pool the leadership team together twice daily to strategize. I learned to prepare my requests for information (RFIs) as the military calls them. Each day after dinner, I would turn the RFIs into the Drill Instructors for answering. Planning and asking clarifying questions set our platoon apart from the others in the company. We always showed up for training on time and with the proper gear. We were no better physically or tactically than our sister platoons; however, our preparation was paramount and set the bar for others to follow. I learned early on that it was the leadership "team" that forged our success. A few years later, I would realize my leadership education started with the three terrific Drill

Instructors I had. They were tough, but they gave a damn about every one of us and wanted us to be successful.

Though you might be in charge, it takes a leadership "team" to be successful. Some people believe this means surrendering authority; it doesn't. If you're in charge, then you already have the authority, and you are responsible for everything that happens, good or bad. Giving leaders the power to make decisions within the rules and scope of the mission only makes you a better leader.

I didn't know any of this as an 18-year old completing Infantry training; this is part of the educational leadership process that takes time and is gained through experience. Clear and concise direction is the key to success. Leadership is not a popularity contest and sometimes can feel like a lonely business. Tough decisions will put a strain on you, and you should not take pleasure in demoting or firing someone unless their conduct is inexcusable or is causing a safety concern to your organization. The choices you make impact more than yourself, and you should take care and consideration in these decisions. Later on, you will read about trusting your instincts; this will be helpful in your decision-making.

Leadership is about being there with your people and embracing the tough times when it's really hard. Does that mean you can't be a forward-thinker and grow your business? Of course not, somebody has to be out there beating the bush, trying to expand the business opportunities. Make yourself available and learn what your keys to success are.

My business has expanded because we always try to do a little more. Growth doesn't mean getting away from what makes you great but just trying to move to the next step. Keep expanding on what you're great at and work on those things you do well. A friend of mine is a retired Delta Force operator whose 25-year military career reads like a Jason Bourne novel. He once told me that, "He didn't need men to do one thing great; he needed men who will do everything great!"

Doing things "great" takes practice and repetition. You have to want to be a little better every day. You can be happy with a day's performance, but you should not be satisfied. It's a fine line that all the best in life, regardless of business, sports, politics, acting, clergy, military, etcetera, have mastered. Mastery takes time; it takes incredible will power, and it takes determination and focus.

The Take-Away

Don't be afraid to lead if put in a leadership position. Don't change who you are; do what you do best. Ask questions, and most importantly, know when to speak and know when to listen, which should be at least twice as often as speaking.

Whatever your leadership style, use positive motivation to lead the way!

BELIEVE IN YOURSELF

We all know the mind controls the body, and you need to believe in yourself and trust in your abilities. Yes, you will second-guess yourself from time to time, and weighing different options and outcomes is healthy, to a point. Believing in yourself means to trust your judgment and confidence in your training, experience, and education. Just reading this book, you are making yourself a better leader! The best leaders know they don't know everything and are continually trying to improve and refine their leadership ability and skill. Even if you do already know everything in this book, the best leaders realize that "reminding" is just as important as knowing.

How do you believe in yourself? It starts with how you feel. As Colonel Keirsey says, "A good day starts with good Physical Training!" By getting out there nearly every day doing something physical, it will naturally produce the proper endorphins to help you "believe in you." It's a scientific fact that the heart and brain are connected to send positive signals to one another. Physical activity is a positive stimulus. Secondly, you must become proficient at your work. You must know your work from an individual standpoint and then must be able to execute that work on time.

It comes down to you, how you feel about yourself and your abilities. By working out regularly, continuing to master your training and education, you are strengthening your decision-making ability and will be able to make assessments based on what you know and your experiences.

Part of believing in you is saying, "Today is a new day!" If yesterday wasn't your best, that day is over, start new; it's time to press on! Keep a running log of events and compile a review for yourself every few days or after critical functions. Don't make this lengthy; a simple three areas to sustain and three areas to improve are all that's needed. If you over complicate this list, you will become overwhelmed with anxiety. If you dwell in the facts of the bad, you will consistently attack your belief in yourself. Use what you've learned (both positive and negative) to ignite your new day! In my life-coaching business, I find that plenty of leaders and executives make a detailed plan; however, they fail to track the outcomes and performance. When it comes time for them to recap on their wins and losses, there's no quantifiable data. Without data, you dwell on what happened most recently. It's not enough to have a vision and direction; you must track how you are doing.

Finally, you must focus on doing it right. This isn't a time for slacking. If it looks and feels like a shortcut, it probably is. If you're a new leader, there's no special snowflake. What I mean by that is, regardless of where you graduated from or who your parents might be, you're expected to work long hours and put in the work.

Hone your craft in the less visible places; plan,

prepare and execute what needs to be done. Learn from your wins and losses and let this assist you in making sound and timely decisions moving forward. Drive your leadership in the right direction.

The Take-Away

Trust in your abilities and your training. Remember, training is a life-long process!
Note three sustains and three improvements per event in your leadership log.
Don't let the highs get too high, or the low's get too low.

Don't Quit

Volunteering for the Army Rangers was an undertaking, and I had no pre-conceived notion on how I would measure up. Before I could even think of donning the coveted Army Ranger Beret, I had to pass Basic and Advanced Training, Airborne School, and then RIP, or formerly known as Ranger Indoctrination Program.

Looking back 30 plus years later, one of the reasons I made it in the Rangers was the foundation built by the Drill Instructors throughout Infantry Training. I was lucky to have such men who cared enough to teach, inspire, motivate, and kick my butt when needed. I remember one particular event we had to do was the rope climb. Outside our old, World War II barracks was a platform that held two ropes about six feet apart and each 30 feet in the air. Not only did you have to climb to the top using the rope and slap the crossbeam with your hand, but also you had to do it in the time standard designated by Drill Sergeant Clark. In a nutshell Drill Sergeant Clark could out-run, out-jump, out-climb, out-shoot, out-push-up, out-road march and of course, out-rope climb anyone in the platoon. I thought he was invincible and we used to say he would drink lighter fluid instead of coffee and piss jet-fuel. Now that last part is a little exaggerated, but as young Soldiers in the Army, Clark was the specimen. If we were wet and hungry, he was wet and hungry, except he never let being wet or hungry bother him.

I was in the final weeks of Infantry Training, and for the most part, looking and acting like a Soldier. I was scoring well on all the requirements for graduation but could not seem to master the rope climb within the time limit. I was getting to the top, but nearly to exhaustion. One evening before he left for his quarters, Drill Sergeant Clark called me out to the rope climb. He said, "You're not locking your feet correctly, and you need to grab the rope as high as you can every pull. Work on it; you'll get there." With that, he got in his car and drove off into the night. I was a little in awe because it was the first time I'd ever heard him use a normal tone of voice.

Every evening, during the few moments we had to ourselves, I would go outside and practice the rope climb. Finally, after weeks of practicing, I made it within the time limit! I remember hitting the ground and beginning some silent, and rather corny, victory dance; spouting off a silent, "Yes! Yes! Yes!" and fist pumping as if I'd hit the lottery! I recall then composing myself and briskly walking back to the barracks to get ready for "lights out."

Thinking no one was the wiser, at breakfast the next day I was walking to my seat in the chow hall and had to pass the table where all the Drill Instructors sat. No one looks at them; you just keep walking as quickly as possible and hope nothing's hanging out of your pocket or a snot on your face that will cause them to stop you! "Speezeeo!" shouted Drill Sergeant Clark. I thought, *oh no, what did I do?* "Yes, Drill Sergeant?" I replied. He said, "Nice job on the rope climb; it's about time!" Startled and bewildered a bit, and thinking *that S.O.B. was watching me*, I said, *"Uh, thank you, Drill Sergeant."* As I started moving to my seat to enjoy my maximum time allotted three-minute breakfast, Drill Sergeant Clark barks out one more thing, "But work on that victory dance, that was awful!" Though I cracked a small smile, I knew if I laughed, I would be doing push-ups for the next two days. I replied, "Roger that Drill Sergeant, Roger that!"

I tell you this story because a task as simple as the rope climb instilled something in me that I always talk about, the "No Quit" philosophy. Now, Drill Sergeant Clark's rope climb wasn't a graduation requirement for Infantry School (we sure didn't know that at the time), but it was HIS personal test for Infantry. A test that compiled mental, physical, and emotional attributes all in one. He knew this, and it was why he made our platoon do it. I carried this "No Quit" and "Never Give Up" philosophy into the rest of my military career and life. My attitude became one of, *I'm not quitting today!*

I wasn't going to worry about tomorrow, but today, *I'm not quitting.* Then the next day I'd say the same thing, and so on.

Ranger Indoctrination Program was one of the single most grueling and challenging courses I've ever attended in my military career. I'd had only about six months in the Army, was barely 18-years-old and fresh out of Airborne School. I was an Army "newbie," and now I'm attempting to join one of the fiercest and most audacious fighting forces in the U.S. military arsenal. I had no idea what to expect or what I was in for; there were nearly 150 candidates in this course, and the Senior Instructor made it clear the first day that he didn't care if any of us made it.

I remember looking around and seeing men bigger, stronger, faster, and older than me and saying to myself; *How am I going to make it through this?* Then it came back to me, the rope climb, and *No Quit!* Every day throughout the four-week course, the size of the group got smaller and smaller. Each morning I'd start with *I'm not quitting today!* Some days were so difficult; I just focused on "making it to lunch!" Each night I celebrated a small victory by saying, "Whew... made it another day!" A company-sized element of 150 men started RIP, a platoon-sized element of 33 graduated, earning the Ranger Beret and the opportunity to serve in the famed 75th Ranger Regiment.

I used this philosophy throughout my military career, and in the dozens of military training courses I was fortunate to attend afterward. Each one had their own level of toughness! My common denominator was the

"No Quit" approach.

The Take-Away

Find a small victory in your life to build on. Do it for yourself! You don't have to prove it to anyone except YOU!
No Quit!

ENGAGE EVERY ROLE FROM WARRIOR TO DIPLOMAT

To be great, as a leader and as an individual, you must engage every role from Warrior to Diplomat. When you master this, you will positively reshape your life. We might think of a warrior as someone such as a Spartan in the Battle of Thermopylae or a Soldier during the D-Day invasion. Alternatively, warrior is defined in the 2015 Merriam-Webster dictionary as *"a person engaged in, experienced in, or devoted to war."* Though these are common themes and ones easily recognizable, they do not entirely define who a warrior is and what makes up their intestinal fortitude.

Many times, the warrior piece is simple; win, defeat the enemy, score the game-winning goal, catch the game-winning pass, or make the big sell. For many of the professional athletes we work with, this is defined as the *"Sports Center"* moment. We like the warrior piece; in fact, we love it. Americans are fascinated by instant success, yet most often it's the day in and day out practice that leads to victory. Getting the big business deal, selling the most products, being recognized; this is the juice or the action, that drives many of us.

Fact: Warriors come in all shapes, sizes, colors, and creeds. A warrior is someone who wants to be the best at what they do and does this by being proficient in their particular craft and doing it consistently. Bus driver, school teacher, mail clerk, flight attendant, doctor, lawyer, business student, Soldier, Sailor, author, actor, radio host, etcetera, you get the picture. Being a warrior is being GREAT at what you do, but this is not enough. To be great, to be the very best, you must be able to engage every role from Warrior to Diplomat effectively.

I remember as a young Army Ranger watching a Navy SEAL who was not the poster-boy of SEAL fitness. He was in his 40s, a little overweight and looked, well, "average." You can imagine my amazement as he climbed an assault ladder into a hovering helicopter faster than any of us, much younger, better-fit (we thought) Army Rangers. His skill as a shooter and assault team leader made us seem we'd just graduated Basic Training. My Squad Leader looked at us and said, "Take notice, boys, that's a warrior!"

Later in my Ranger days, we had a civilian show up at the gun range to teach us combat shooting. Again, here we are, trained, skilled Rangers who live their lives by the code of fitness and marksmanship, able to do things with their hands and weapons better than every comparable unit in the world. Big Jim (or whatever his real name was) shows up, all 270-pounds of him, tobacco in his lip, and with a deep southern drawl we could barely understand. As you can imagine, we looked at each other and said, "Who is this guy?" He goes on a synopsis of shooting covering cues and techniques to improve accuracy and control. I remember not really paying much attention until he squeezes the trigger on the Beretta pistol putting all 13 rounds on the target in a circle the size of a silver dollar, while still giving us instruction. The proof was in the pudding, and as you can imagine, we listened attentively the rest of the day. Once again, another warrior in a different shape and size.

The warrior role is the easiest to recognize because it contains tangible feedback. However, it's all the roles you'll be expected to take part in that will define you. Sometimes our skills are genuinely talented-related. All of us are born with different levels of talent, and we refine these talents by our expertise; the practice and skills we put in. You all know people who are "naturals," who have God-given talent with which they are born. Some use these talents to be successful while others waste them by never fully developing them because the practice is hard, and must be evolved. It's everything else you do, which defines you. The hard work behind the scenes, the teamwork, the commitment, the honor, the integrity, the mentoring, the coaching; this is what embodies the warrior principles.

If you want to be GREAT at what you do, you must be able to communicate this to others positively. You must check your ego not only at the door but do it each day! You must know you're not the smartest person in the room, and if you are, you better hire someone smarter! You must be passionate about what you do and must be dedicated to the hard work it's going to take to get there. Keep in mind there are no shortcuts to excellence! You must be able to say, "I won't let my mate down, today or any day." Sometimes we are recognized for these great achievements, but most times we are not. Find yourself a mentor, learn from someone else, keep learning throughout your career; it's never too late to start. Remember, "Iron sharpens iron!"

A good friend of mine is a superstar professional hockey player, and he exemplifies the warrior to diplomat philosophy. He has earned countless personal and team awards, Gold Medals, championships, and his star quality is known all over North America and Europe. His focus and intensity to his craft are well-documented. What makes him so special is not just the warrior focus during training and competition, rather it's his ability to sell his sport by showing his true humility both in and out of competition. I've personally watched him stop and take time to talk to fans, adults, children, and up and coming players who are in awe, seeing and talking to their "hero." I've watched him have a conversation with an 11-year-old about the youth game he played, asking the young boy the details of the plays he made. It was truly fascinating and humbling. Though he lives a busy schedule, he takes the time to be a diplomat, understanding it's just as important as the performance part, maybe even more so.

I spent the majority of 2008 in Afghanistan as a Sergeant Major training the Afghan military. My gunfighter role, one that I was uniquely trained and equipped for, was minimal. However, my leader, coach, mentor, medic, schoolteacher, repairman, etc.

roles were lengthy. I learned more about myself and my real character than I ever did before. This was, without a doubt, one of my most challenging assignments, and it wasn't because of intense combat action. This assignment bothered me for many years because we could only measure the process in very, very small increments. But then, as I became older and wiser, it dawned on me. Yes, I was a Soldier, and though I was more suited for battle, I learned a valuable lesson of making a difference in countless others regardless of what role you've been assigned to play.

I use this experience now to tell all those I life-coach, "be a superstar in the role asked of you!" The moral of this story is simple, be the best at any role required of you and be able to perform equally in many of them. Smile when it's time to smile. Sell when it's time to sell. Mentor when it's time to mentor. Be a warrior, be a diplomat, be everything in between.

The Take-Away

As leaders, to engage every role from Warrior to Diplomat, sometimes you must do things that frankly aren't noticed nor will ever get seen. It's not what you get recognized for that defines you; it's what you do that's right, even when it doesn't get noticed, that makes you legendary.

You can train on quantifiable tasks to be the warrior; to be the diplomat takes qualitative attributes you build up over time.

Not all jobs are stimulating. However, they are all important, and there are no short cuts to excellence, ever!

LEADERS MUST BE ADAPTABLE

As a leader, you must be adaptable to what's happening in order to extinguish job fires (in the figurative sense) which can ultimately take place several times a week. You must be able to prevent issues through proper planning, cross-training, and the knack and familiarity to see what's coming. The best leaders prevent intensities, fight them quickly and calmly when they do arise, and never fuel the flames with such things as emotion, gossip, or an agenda.

Let's look at actual Firefighters, the brave men and women who do this for a living. When they respond to a fire, do they immediately rush in? Do firefighters ever act like they are not in control? Of course not, they arrive at the situation and quickly assess what's going on. They look at the fire and see its patterns and where the best place is to enter. They create holes for the smoke to ventilate, and they spray water in specific locations to prevent the fire from spreading, as well as to protect their teammates who may have to enter the blaze. They quickly assess, quickly plan, communicate the message, and then go. Calm, cool, collected and detailed. A term used in military special operations in reference to speed and moving is known as "slow is smooth and smooth is fast." This means you are not just charging in blindly, rather moving at a speed that travels you quickly and safely to the next event. This can and should be used in any business model.

Non-adaptable leaders are easy to point out because these types start fires by lack of respect, personal courage, chatter, innuendos, and their basic absence (or trust) of their own abilities. Avoid these leaders; they will drag you down. If you work for a leader like this, you can combat their actions by being in the fire prevention business: be prepared and plan accordingly.

The other type of leader, the firefighter, seldom gets rattled in the face of conflict, deadlines, or even insurmountable odds. They can take criticism from above and below, dissect what is necessary, and then adapt appropriately to give those under their charge sound and timely direction to complete the task. Granted, this takes training through experience and being proficient in your field. Keeping control of yourself and your emotions is the most critical first step!

You have to prepare for the unexpected. This takes a lot more work, but as you gain institutional knowledge, you will be able to prevent many fires before they start. When I needed an answer, I'd often ask the team. You'll find there are many with great knowledge of situations through past experiences in business and life. Find the subject matter experts or ask the employee who has been there for an extended period. You will be pleasantly surprised that many times this information is already self-absorbed inside your organization. I often, when planning a project, ask the team, "what haven't I thought of?" or "what am I forgetting?" or "what would you add to ensure our success?" Most times, someone will chime in with something that can assist you in adapting and moving forward.

Adaptable is not just a cool modern term; it's a life choice that today's leaders need to make if they want to stay relevant. I talk with leaders about how professional sports are moving towards what they call a new breed of coach. Generally, this coach is younger in age, and they may say this coach is an "offensive genius" or "systems guru" or use similar terms. Really the playbook part of sports and business is relatively the same, but what some of these younger coaches understand is the mind of the "athlete." You, as a business leader, need to understand the mind of your employee as well. People are motivated by different things, and some athletes, for example, can care less what's on the front of the jersey. They are playing for their name on the back. Maybe this can be viewed as selfish, but it's how some people feel. To achieve the maximum performance out of those under your charge, you must work at these three things:

- Understand who they are as humans and what motivates them.
- Encourage them to keep their personal or specific reasons in the "proper place," so it doesn't affect the group.
- Employ a healthy work environment.

When I mention encouraging others to keep their reasons in their proper place, it is meant to reinforce that their particular motivation should remain private and not openly shared where it might form jealousy or cause strife. I talked recently with a former NFL quarterback who played mostly in the late 1970s and 80s. He said when he played; no one talked about salaries and what everyone was being paid. It was not open source information as it today and just was not discussed so as not to cause any contention.

My point is simple. As a modern-day leader, you must be adaptable to understand human dynamics. This does not mean you lower the bar. This means you have to properly communicate what is expected to your team. Start at the group level then to each individual as necessary.

Trust me; all your hard work is going to be worth it! Being calm, cool, collected, capable, and adaptable when work flares up are the most effective keys to success. Get on task, give sound and timely advice, and get the job completed the most expedient way possible. You can do it.

The Take-Away

Be a firefighter and not a fire starter by controlling your emotions.
Plan accordingly for the job and also for contingencies.
Adapt, overcome, learn, and be productive.

Mental Toughness

Toughness is one of the most challenging and critical

attributes to sustain in any of us. Let's be clear; toughness is not a trait you are born with. It is neither talent nor genetic makeup. Sure, some of these skills may be imprinted on you as a youth from your primary caregiver; however, just because your parents were "tough" doesn't mean you will be tough. Toughness is a "learned" trait and can happen at any time in your life. Some of us learn sooner than others through events or challenges in our lives; some of us learn it later. The bottom line, if you think you're not tough enough, it's just because you haven't discovered it yet.

Toughness is simply the ability to "bounce back" in the face of adversity. It's the ability to handle situations with calm and clarity while keeping emotions in check. Toughness has nothing to do with being mean, cold, callous, or insensitive. I always chuckle when people with those qualities are labeled as "tough." They're not tough; they are bullies or other words that describe the impervious nature of these types.

People who work in specific jobs are sometimes thought of as tough: law enforcement, firefighters, paramedics, military, and even teachers. Toughness has to do with dealing with difficult situations, environments, or even people. A good friend of mine is retired from the Air Force, and he always says, "You Army guys are tough. I couldn't sleep in the mud!" The reality is he is just as tough as us "Army grunts" but doesn't have to suck-up some of the adverse conditions; though I'm confident he could if he had to.

Toughness comes from learning to struggle and then emerge. Toughness is learning there are no shortcuts to excellence, and success is often disguised as dull, un-dignified, hard work! It's accomplishing goals with honor, integrity, and personal courage; keeping your goals in a clear vision and not trampling over people in the process. It has nothing to do with haste; hesitation requires you to take risks. Toughness is having the ability to be out-front if need be, proactive, and the understanding that you can take two steps backward as long as you're always taking three steps forward. Toughness knows your positive reputation takes determination and persistence, combined with the moral high ground to do what's right even if it's unpopular. You build your toughness through positive beliefs in yourself and your goals. Your goals have to be moral and ethical and the foundation for who you are. Some people are categorized as harsh because they are verbally short, extraordinarily opinionated, and come off as aggressive. This is not a tough person; this is a socially unapproachable person who needs to work on their humility.

I had a chance to meet a CFO of one of the largest global companies who was known as a financial genius. The company he worked for is a leader in their market, and he was described to me as having both a "shark and volcano" leadership style. He would swallow people up quickly and ravage them for remarks or statements he didn't agree with and would listen to a point and then explode. Walking with a few of his employees to meet him, I noticed they were uncomfortable, and one was fidgety. Immediately I thought, "Who are we going to meet? Darth Vader?" After his underling's description of him, I wasn't concerned about the short meet and greet, already sensing the CFO would not be the type to hire professional leadership training for his group as he was described as someone who "had all the answers." The greeting lasted about two minutes in the hallway of an airport. The CFO was relatively courteous to me, though you could tell this quick gathering was "taking time out of his day." After the introduction by one of his staff, I gave my 30-second elevator pitch. He took my card and went on his way. He had his staff all in lockstep as they made their way to baggage claim. (It actually reminded me of the scene in Christmas Vacation where Clark Griswold's boss and all of his flunkies are marching through the office.) I thanked the gentleman who had set up the introduction. He shook my hand and said, "I told you he's tough." I looked at him and said, "Thanks for the intro, but that's not toughness."

Toughness comes in all shapes and sizes; from people like Mother Theresa, Ranger Michael Schlitz, Patricia G. Spisso, Special Forces Captain Ben Harrow, to the college graduate working two jobs to pay off their student loans, riding the bus because they can't yet afford a car. Toughness knows that people just won't give you free stuff, and if your current situation needs it, you're working even harder for your path to interdependence. Toughness is not a tool for doing less, and toughness knows if you can't afford it right now, then don't buy it.

Material items do not make you tough; they make you a person with a lot of material stuff! Toughness is answering the call at three o'clock in the morning from a friend who needs a ride, and it's an hour out of your way, and then letting your friend know the following day they need to make better decisions. Toughness is being responsible, accountable, committed, and knowing you have to be able to push through adversity. It knows how to lean on those trusted agents for help, but also knows you have your own personal duty for success.

Toughness has everything to do with responsibility and accountability of yourself, first and foremost. The famous saying from President Harry S. Truman of "The buck stops with me," is the definition of those with toughness. Accept responsibility for your actions and be capable and knowledgeable enough to know. If you're not sure what you're accountable for, then have the responsibility to ask!

Toughness knows you cannot walk over people for your success, and if you do, you will always be labeled as something else. Those who are tough believe and trust in others, take them at their word, and use the term "fool me once, shame on you; fool me twice then shame on me." Tough people always, I mean always, give others second chances (sometimes even a third).

Tough people always want to win but realize that losses are a part of learning and how you handle loss is what will define you. Tough people use the terminology I borrowed from my friend and legendary Special Forces warrior Sergeant Major Pat Fensom, "Get mad. Get pissed off if you want to. But, get over it, and most importantly, get on with it!" Finding the right balance of emotion is the key to success. Use the loss, the negative, the setback, to fuel your fire to get back after it. When tackling adversity, find ways to simplify your life and take something off your plate. It's okay to say "no" once in a while. Focus on what you need to do to get yourself back into the game of life and back on your primary objective. This is what tough people do; this is what you can do.

My toughness is still building and growing, and I'm not done yet. We learn toughness, we adjust, and we use humility, honor, and a belief in ourselves and those around us to build the necessary foundation. Toughness is knowing, and most importantly realizing, that life has its share of challenges that will test your emotional and physical spirit. It's the ability to lean on your family or very close friends when you need your own personal "boost" of motivation and finding your way through the storms. Toughness gives you the necessary belief in yourself, your abilities and does so with character as the keystone. Remember, if you think you're not tough enough, you can still learn it.

The Take-Away

You are not born with a level of toughness; it is a learned behavior.

Toughness has nothing to do with being mean, cold, callous, or insensitive.

Toughness is defined as the ability to "bounce back" after adversity.

Trust Your Instincts

Instincts in Webster's dictionary are defined as

1: a natural or inherent aptitude, impulse, or capacity
<had an instinct for the right word>
2: a largely inheritable and unalterable tendency of an
organism to make a complicated and specific response
to environmental stimuli without involving reason
b: behavior that is mediated by reactions below the
conscious level (Merriam-Webster, 2015)

We all have instincts of some sort; no different than the animal in the woods that uses them for daily survival; we all have a natural level. Instincts are honed through experience and even a little skepticism. You've heard the adage that if *"something sounds too good to be true, it usually is."* Those are our instincts which tell us that someone is trying to sell us a worthless bag of goods, or the "no money down" on something is loaded with interest penalties. Soldiers have instincts in battle, *"do I bound left for the attack, or should I go right?"* Many times, it's instincts that give us the right course of action, and a few times, it's a calculated guess, but our action often comes from experience and that "inner feel."

Instincts provide a cause and course of action. If you have been doing something for a long time, it's easy to get the "feel" for what's happening. Just like a seasoned coach might know the right play to call based on the fact they have been diagraming and calling plays for 20 years. Or a stockbroker has the "feel" for a certain stock because they know the performance history, who is managing the fund or running the company. Experts have scientific proof that the brain controls instinct; however, many times, we feel it in our stomach, rib cage, or gut as they say. Some have coined this as an "inner ding," and if you have to talk yourself into something, it's usually not the right idea. My point in this chapter is to trust those instincts, listen to them and what they're telling you, and use them in your planning process.

I was preparing to leave Afghanistan in early 2009. I had about 15 months before my retirement and one final assignment in the Army. I campaigned for a few higher-profile jobs at a couple of military bases, and though some were promising, nothing was really turning out. I was presented with a position at a military base in New York, and though it was a long shot, it looked encouraging, and I thought I'd apply. My interview went very well, and it looked as if my orders would be accepted and produced from Department of the Army. I was, of course, excited yet a little anxious. My instincts told me that this job wasn't right for me, and though I was highly qualified, it would be a stretch to receive as this was a very prestigious position. A few days before I was to report, the Army personnel office informed me that another Sergeant Major was chosen for the position. My gut instinct was right. I received an assignment for a position in Garrison Operations at Fort Monmouth, NJ instead. Though still a Sergeant Major position, it came with far less fan-fare and pres-tige as the other job. Though I knew nothing about this job or the scope of the work, my instincts said, "it was going to be alright."

As it turned out, this final assignment was better than I could have imagined, one that I look back on as truly wonderful from a personal and professional standpoint. I had incredible mentorship from two great leaders, Lieutenant Colonel (Retired) John Occhipinti and Command Sergeant Major (Retired) Lou Benevides, who set me up for success and supported me in moving on to my current career by preparing me to look outside the box. I was able to get physically healthy, complete my education, reunite with my family and friends, as well as learn a myriad of new skills that set me up for triumph today.

The Take-Away

Trust your instincts. It's a proven fact that your instincts are necessary for your success.
Everything happens for a reason. Trust and believe!
Sometimes you just have to go with it!

Subject Matter Experts (SMEs)

If you're like me, and you want to keep improving, then find the ones who "know the know." These are the men and women on the ground we call the *subject matter experts*. These folks live it, breath it, know it, and understand it. The best leaders look, listen, and ask plenty of questions. They find out what works and what doesn't. Do your internal evaluation and process and find out why something is not getting done. For example, is it a lack of energy of the team or are you fighting an old system? One of the most critical steps in leadership is finding the root cause of the problem; you do this, and usually, the solution is relatively simple.

When I began this journey over a decade ago to write a book, it was an area in which I was unfamiliar. As I began the research, I found the many ways one can publish a book, from traditional publishing to self-publishing, tips on how to pitch your book to publishers, the processes, writing a query letter, and on and on. I will tell you that I became overwhelmed with how and what to do and really had no institutional knowledge to lean on. I even asked a few colleagues about what they did, only to become more confused on the procedures. But with anything, if you want to be great, you need to dive in and find authority, the SME!

After years of really senseless research, I took a page out of my own manual and reconnected with a great military friend who is a very successful businessman and author. We hadn't talked for years, but the great thing about military camaraderie is it never goes away. When we finally were back in touch, we were talking as if it was 20 years ago. My friend and former teammate, Steve, walked me through the process step by step, what he did and how he was published, not leaving out a detail, and breaking it down in the simplest of terms. I could feel the fire inside of me burning, and once again, I was on this quest for accomplishment. After several meaningful and educational phone calls and e-mails, my friend said to me, "now it's time for the real expert" and put me on with the editor who's assisted me at seeing this through to fruition!

Caren took me on as a client, and from the first day, I listened attentively, took copious notes, and put in my personal work to show her I was serious and not taking this opportunity lightly. Caren is the SME, so I used her instruction and guidance to formulate the necessary plan for completion. My sincere thanks will never be enough!

It's not enough to find the expert; you must do your research to find the "right expert." Knowledge is one thing, but the right SME will be able to present that information to you in simple ways that you can understand, and then implement. A few years ago, when I was doing evaluations on professional players prior to the draft, I asked a pro scout to explain to me the measures he uses in his evaluation. He said to me, "You won't understand it." I replied, "Then you don't know it well enough." Of course, that caught an eye roll, but at the end of the day I was right, and he was either too arrogant or not qualified at his job. I've always enjoyed the famous quote Albert Einstein is credited with, "If you can't explain it to a 6-year-old, you don't understand it well enough."

We all love the "comfort zone;" doing the things we know we are good at or the things we can do easily from just memory. It's a natural aspect of the way we are wired. Nobody wants to look like a fool, especially in front of others. The problem with comfort zones is they actually get smaller if you do not step outside of them. All the best leaders want to be challenged. They find the experts to help, they ask questions and let the experts show them how to do it, regardless of rank or position.

When I was a Ranger Platoon Sergeant in 1ST Ranger Battalion back in the 1990s, I distinctly remember a day during a training exercise when the Ranger Regimental Commander asked one of our young Ranger Privates how to operate a new machine gun we just got into our inventory. Now the Ranger Regimental Commander is "God" to Rangers, and Colonel David L. Grange was no exception.

Before commanding the Rangers, Colonel Grange commanded the Army unit commonly known as Delta Force. I tell you this because it's relevant to the story. Here is this senior military Officer, taking a knee in the woods next to a 19-year-old Ranger who has been trained and qualified on a new machine gun and saying, "Ranger, show me how this works." The young Ranger complied and spent the next few minutes going through loading, unloading, functions check, and of course, firing the machine gun. The lesson didn't stop here. Colonel Grange looked at the young Ranger and said, "Ok Ranger, now put me through the battle drill, and don't cut me any slack!" The young Ranger put the Colonel through the drills as if he were training a recruit. This went on for the next 20 minutes until the Colonel was confident he could engage the enemy with this weapon. The likelihood he would use this machine gun in battle was slim, but he was never the kind of man to not be prepared and wanted to know all the requirements of his men.

Know what your people are doing and how they are doing it. If you don't know something, ask the right questions and find those who do know, even if you are the boss and the person who knows is one of the youngest in the organization. This takes humility, courage, and respect. Society changes, business changes, the way we fight wars changes. The best leaders are adaptable to those situations and never use the term, *"this is how we always do it!"* Colonel Grange did exactly what great leaders do by continuing to learn!

The Take-Away

The key to solving problems is to find the root cause of the problem; ask the right questions!

If you are the expert, know how to explain what you know in simple terms.

Leadership requires you to listen and learn at every level. You have to be adaptable enough to want to learn.

FORCE MULTIPLIER

I often get asked the question, what's the single piece of advice you can give a leader? This is a great question! I talk about having honor and character throughout this book and standing up for the men and women under your charge; making hard decisions and knowing that sometimes leadership is a lonely place. However, if I had to tell a leader just one thing, I'd ask them to be a "force multiplier!"

The United States Department of Defense defines Force multiplier as:

"A capability that, when added to and employed by a combat force, significantly increases the combat potential of that force and thus enhances the probability of successful mission accomplishment."

Although the definition implies military action, I actually feel this term has more value in the non-military sense. You, as the leader, are a combat leader in your own right and you can plug the force multiplier definition into your job and your role as a manager. There will be many times when the specific and exact answer will not be available, and trusting your instincts, as well as training and experience, will be necessary. However, being positive, calm under pressure, not over-hyping what's happening, and being a voice of reason will make the actual difference; this is being a force multiplier! Your attitude, your focus, your spirit is the force multiplier!

I've been fortunate to serve in many great units in the military and work with amazing businesses and sports teams. Many times, a particular group went from good to great or even from great back to good with the single change of one key leader. You can be a good organization, but you can become a great one when the leader is a force multiplier! The personnel didn't change; it was the same group from previous years. However, the new leader, new coach, new manager, would keep the razor's edge of the people focused in the vital direction.

During my tour in 1st Ranger Battalion, we had a Battalion Commander who epitomized the force multiplier ethos. His name was Lieutenant Colonel Brian Pentecost, and he was one of the finest Army Commanders I've ever had the pleasure of serving under. Colonel Pentecost was an extremely bright man who would fool you with his deep southern drawl, tobacco in his lip, and his pleasure in the hunting of game animals. I distinctly remember one morning him pulling up in his pick-up truck to the Battalion Headquarters with a dead deer in the bed of his vehicle, drops of blood on the bumper. The Colonel shot and dressed a buck at first light and still made it to physical training on time.

He knew everyone's name and was a stickler for details, especially when it came to training. His mind was focused on the mission, preparing our unit for combat and he knew we were the tip of the fighting spear for our great Nation. I remembered the Colonel sitting, during a training briefing, never taking a note, and asking a specific question to a junior Officer about a single event on a particular day after listening for over an hour! We would look at each other with amazement and wonder. How had he remembered to ask that granular level of detail question?

I don't believe I'd ever seen him upset or even remember him being upset; if he was, we never heard about it. Though I was not new to the Ranger Regiment, this was my first tour being in this particular Ranger Battalion. During a Battalion level physical fitness event, where all 500+ Rangers are present, he called me out in front of the Battalion to recite a stanza of the Ranger Creed, which was a mandatory memorization script by every man in the unit. It was unexpected; no one told me prior he was going to call upon me, and though slightly nervous, I recited the stanza flawlessly, verbatim and led the unit in a set of exercises.

Throughout the next two years under his command, our Ranger Battalion became one of the most lethal, spirited, and dedicated fighting forces on this planet. His focus was on the Rangers, our mission, and our ability to launch anywhere in the world in 18 hours or less to combat the enemies of our Country. Calm, collected, smart, agile, caring, friendly, with a sense of humor, are words which described Colonel Pentecost. More importantly, he brought a sense of being genuinely thrilled for what he was doing. He wasn't the cheerleader or the "rah-rah" type, but you knew he loved being our commander. Not for personal gain or promotion, but for the sense of honor of leading brave warriors. Colonel Pentecost set the standard for being a force multiplier.

The Take-Away

Force multiplier starts with a positive attitude! Control what you can control. Be calm, cool, and collected in the face of conflict. If you have to get upset, do it privately, get over it, and get on with it.

COACHING, INSPIRING, AND MENTORING IN LEADERSHIP

There are so many facets to leadership that many times we forget the most important ones are coaching, inspiring, and mentoring. It's a given if you're a business leader or a coach of a sports team that you must be proficient in the skill set needed for success. These are often called the Xs and Os, the mastery of the playbook. Many believe this is enough to be successful; that personality and personal relations don't matter, and as long as "I'm the smartest person in the room," then that should be enough. The best leaders and coaches out there know they are not the smartest person in the room, and even if they are, they never let on to that fact. I've given you some personal examples of leaders like this. Bottom line, there is always someone smarter! As you rise in positions of authority and responsibility, your particular skill set must continue to refine based on your experiences and your proficiency moving onward. You must be able to look at the bigger picture. As you increase your responsibility, your requirement to look at all facets of your business will surge.

I like to use a 100 percent measure in describing the requirements for coaching, mentoring, inspiring, and X and O capability in the leadership formula. Coaching, mentoring, and inspiring each takes a 30% gate in leadership for 90% of the pie. You have to be able to adequately do all three of these as a leader if you want success for your organization. The days of the "my way or the highway" leadership style, or being a non-communicator because those under your charge should be "thankful they have a job," are not only archaic attitudes, but will never produce the best results. Don't get me wrong, in no way am I suggesting you have to coddle employees or athletes because doing this has its own sets of challenges. I'm merely stating that you must be equally great (30% each) at all three facets of these leadership traits for the best success to take place.

Finally, the last 10% is the playbook; the Xs and Os. This is the technical and execution portion that makes your organization or your team successful. Please do not take this 10% lightly thinking it's not that important because its only 10% of the equation. It's the percentage that can define victory. This can't just be an 8% or 9% effort; your 10% must be specific, detailed, planned accordingly, and your organization or team must clearly understand it.

Watch a championship sporting event, and you'll see that many times the competitors are so equal it comes down to the coach who has mastered this 10%. How you explain the 10%, with details (charts, video, personal explanations), will delineate you. It all comes down to being GREAT at the previous three attributes in coaching, mentoring, and inspiring.

Coaching is a term or a skill set that we've all done, and still do at some point nearly every day. From showing our children how to properly tie their shoes when they are young to assisting a new intern in updating their resume or even advising a senior partner in the importance of masterful conversations, coaching is key to any successful organization. The term "you can't teach an old dog new tricks" doesn't apply to the coaching portion of leadership. It would be best if you continued to better yourself through education and training and show those under your charge that the keystone for their success is through their personal development as well. The best way to "coach" this is by doing, or as we commonly say, using the "lead by example" leadership philosophy. Showing the importance of continuing education sets the standard and improves readiness.

Another critical part is being consistent in your actions and your rules; wavering standards equals no standards. You don't need to be a volcano. Instead, you need to be stable, dependable, and reliable in your decision-making. I know a head coach who doesn't allow TV's in the team gymnasium; not just turned off, not present at all. It's his rule, and he doesn't get concerned if it's unpopular. He has a clear directive that he wants the athletes in the gym to focus on their workout and not be distracted by anything else.

Also, what you cannot do in this portion is lack personal and group communication. I've said it many times in this book so far, and I will reiterate it once again, you must be a great communicator! Make it a point to talk to as many of your employees or team as you can every day! Know their first names, where they are from, their family, and their background. (I am not asking you to invade on their personal space, but you must know who they are as a human and what is important to them.) Ask questions, make sure they understand and provide sound and timely feedback. Let people know where they stand from a positive message. Remember, people learn and perceive differently, which will require you to send the same message in different formats often.

Finally, as a coach in the leadership model, you must make corrections; do not wait and watch the same mistakes. When you fail to make corrections, you facilitate the crash of individuals and your team. You don't have to always criticize, but you must let them know what they are doing right and what they need to improve upon. Give them the room to fix it, show it to them from several angles, and ensure your direction is clear and concise. It's OK to have high expectations; in fact, it's necessary if you want to have a top organization. High expectations combined with learning cultivate initiative. If your people aren't adequately coached, they will stagnate, so if something is not getting done the way you expect, take a look internally first. Find those who want to learn and grow and let them excel. Most of us cannot hand pick every person on our team, and even if you have that ability, sometimes your choices don't work out. Play the cards you are dealt and find the appropriate job skill (the talent) for each person.

I often say in my leadership seminars that making a machine gunner a sniper (or vice-versa) is never a quick fix. Just because they both have a weapon that shoots bullets as their primary tool does not mean one can do the other's job accurately, systematically, or to the efficiency you are looking to achieve. If you need someone to change their job description, then give them the proper training first before putting them in an impossible situation. Coaching takes a lifetime of dedication. Your positive reputation takes determination and persistence. If you want to be a great coaching leader, keep learning through stretching and growing yourself!

Inspiring is an attribute often taken for granted, and many times either undervalued or misunderstood. I was fortunate to be mentored by great leaders who were experts in inspiring. Colonel Hank Keirsey was one of them. His ability to take a bad situation and make it positive by encouraging those around him was truly renowned. It didn't matter the obstacle; Colonel Keirsey wanted you to know he cared, and he was willing to do whatever it took to help you and the team succeed. His inspiration was so useful it caused others to individually work harder and push further and faster if the need arose!

You inspire by not only making those around you feel good on individual and group successes but also by giving them the belief that the task can be accomplished. Your inspiration has to be positive, heartfelt, and timely. For lack of a better term, know when and where to give kudos; simple. Also, it has to be REAL!

If you try to fake it, everyone will know, so your inspiration has to be 100% real. If you fail to inspire, you will then, by default, force their passion in weakening.

Some leaders feel they don't have to tell their people when they do something right, only when they are doing something wrong. I had a business professional tell me, "If I'm not correcting my people, they should assume they are doing it right!" I replied, "You actually believe that?" Positive feedback is, at times, even more critical than corrective action. You are not soft or weak by telling someone "Good effort on that project," or "I appreciate your hard work." Everyone brings a certain level of desire to the table, some more than others. It's your job as a leader to bring inspiration and positive motivation to the team. You don't have to be the cheer-leader; instead, you have to be able to show each person that you care.

Mentorship is a term often used in the military to guide and assist other Soldiers with their personal development. It's a big part of the development of leaders, and it was a big part of my own personal and professional life. Mentoring is more than answering the random or occasional question from a subordinate; it's developing open lines of communication and dialogue. The best mentors do not try to create carbon copies of themselves; they assist those being mentored in staying on the right path to success and recognize that everyone must walk in their own steps. Mentoring, like coaching, takes an equal amount of energy. You want to assist those being mentored not to make the same mistakes you've made, but also realize that when mistakes are made, it's a part of life. Being a great mentor is knowing what to say, how to say it, and when to say it. Mentors ask a lot of questions and many times double as therapists because they are great at listening (there we go again on this attribute!). A mentor should be a sculptor, knowing when to mold and knowing when to smooth out the rough edges. A mentor highlights the individual's talents and encourages them to find their path. The right mentor doesn't judge or direct; instead, they guide and show belief. I want to thank all the great mentors in my life who in the past, and still today, assist me in being awesome!

The Take-Away

You need to be equally great at coaching, inspiring, and mentoring, and then add your Xs and Os piece. Continue to develop your abilities. Your leadership and coaching style should "update" every three to five years.
Show people the way, don't always do it for them.

COMMUNICATE

There are leadership consultants who have made an excellent living for themselves by strictly focusing on communication. That's how important it is. We've broken down the definition of communication in many ways and have dissected the meaning into hundreds of components. Here is my simple answer: communication wins wars! Communication gets the project completed on time. Communication makes and sells the best product. Communication wins championships.

If you want to be a great leader, you must be an excellent communicator; being a good communicator is not enough in this day and age. Messages get lost in today's information access society through text messages, e-mails, and other non-verbal transmission. Phone calls and face-to-face communication are diminishing and contributing to the message dilemma.

The number one precedence to being an exceptional communicator is being a **thoughtful listener**. To do this, you have to remove ego from the equation. You must be able to listen without emotion as the primary vehicle. However, emotions will always be present, and to remove them totally will make you cold and callous, which I never recommend. I have found throughout my over three decades of military service and leadership consulting that the leaders who can listen with a "focus" on the intent, are the best at not only analyzing the problem but also quickly finding the right solution to it.

One of the most tremendous communicators I've ever served with is a legendary Infantry Colonel, Mike Anderson. He had this uncanny ability to hear everything that was said and accurately respond to it. One particular situation had us interviewing a young Soldier who was caught up in an online gambling scheme. Here is this young man sitting in the Colonel's office with his entire chain of command and Military Police investigators. I'm confident his mind was racing. He was being asked if he wanted to waive his rights to an attorney. The investigators wanted to ask questions and get to the bottom of this issue (so did his chain of command), and the young man wanted to get any information off his chest just as quickly. However, right before the official questioning began, Colonel Anderson interjected and said, "Son, why do you want to waive your rights? Why don't you want an attorney?" The young man was visibly shaken and thought by answering freely right now; it might somehow lessen his responsibility in the situation. The Colonel and I both suspected it wasn't this young man's plan, he was talked into it by former friends of his, and he was being set up to take the brunt of it. The Colonel asked him again, "Why do you want to waive your rights?" Amid all the chaos, the Colonel was the only one listening to this young man, hearing the nervousness and crackles in his voice. The young man had no answer for wanting to waive his rights, so the Colonel calmly said to his chain of command, "Take this young man down to the JAG office and let him talk to an attorney and then if he wants to waive his rights you can question him." Sound and timely advice from someone who was a great listener! If this young man had waived his rights, his career would have been over, if not worse. However, by getting proper legal advice, it was concluded he was set-up by the schemers, and he was permitted to complete his military commitment honorably. In the haste to "get the answers," there was a failure to listen and decipher what was critical to mission success.

Colonel Anderson would often sit in the back of the room during the weekly academic briefings at our unit. The academic staff (comprised of both civilian and military professors), played a vital role in the development of the future leaders of America and subsequently had an essential voice in selecting those who were going to be sent to West Point and those who were to be sent home. Colonel Anderson thought it was going too far. He felt the academic department was cutting candidates loose too early and slashing numbers so they could focus on the few who they knew would make it. The Colonel was a former professor at West Point himself, and he knew there were systems in place to help those who are academically requiring.

As this meeting was going on, the Academic Team was going back and forth on who they were dismissing. Most everyone (including me) was just nodding our heads and taking notes. Colonel Anderson was the only one listening. As they went over the list for dismissal Colonel Anderson piped in and said, "We are not dismissing anyone in the first semester; we are leaders, teachers, and mentors, and we are going to give these great people the benefit of the doubt." An opinionated senior professor immediately chimed in with some facts on why they needed to dismiss the students during the first semester. He quoted institutional data and was well-spoken about it. The Colonel looked and listened to him directly without interruption. When the professor was finished, Colonel Anderson eloquently said, "I understand your concern and know this will be an additional workload on all of us. That being said, smarter people than we have selected these young men and women to go to West Point. They have achieved, through an incredible evaluation and selection process, to receive an appointment. We must teach them, prepare them, and inspire them. If we do all of that, and they still don't meet the standard, then we will send them home knowing we did everything we could."

There was no response from anyone because the Colonel's communication was nothing less than stellar. He was calm, non-abrasive, and gave a clear and concise marching order to achieve the desired end-state. Colonel Anderson knew we had a group that was highly motivated, educated, and could assist these young men and women on their journey if "we" gave the effort. This was one of the most rewarding military assignments I've ever had for the simple fact I worked for a leader who communicated accurately and at all levels. He was genuine and cared about everyone from the top down to the lowest ranking under his command.

Language Defines Your Leadership

Leadership can be simplified into three terms: purpose, direction, and motivation. All three of these are components of encouragement. As a leader, if you can provide these three simple attributes, you will be successful. That being said, the language you use when giving purpose, direction, and motivation define who you are.

Let me be clear, though this chapter is how to use your language without degrading or cursing, to be realistic most of us at one time or another have used foul language in some type of response. There's even use of some choice words throughout this book, so I'm not saying this is a zero-tolerance lesson. What I will describe to you is how to properly use your language skills, so your point is delivered and received accurately. There might be a time and a place for displays such as a coach's famous table flip in a locker room sending water and sports drinks everywhere with a few choice words, but I'm here to tell you they are few and far between.

I'll never forget standing in the Panamanian jungle, my olive drab jungle fatigues soaked with sweat from military training, having just been promoted to Sergeant by Captain Bernard Champoux, Commander of Bravo Company, 2nd Battalion, 75th Ranger Regiment. A few hours after being promoted in the field, Captain Champoux called all the leadership to the command area in the center of the company perimeter. We were training hard and doing a fine job, but it was just OK, it wasn't great, and Rangers are expected to be boundless. We needed a little kick in the behind from the boss, and Captain Champoux spoke to us directly and sincerely, looking each leader in the eye, and saying what he expected out of each of us. I was afraid to move, and I think everyone was. We were waiting for the boss to turn the speech into some curse-laden football coach speech, but he never did. When someone is yelling and screaming at you, it's easy to shut your brain off and tune them out. However, Captain Champoux's proper use of language, calmly telling us what we needed to do, and never once cursing at us, got his point across. Wow, did it ever! From this forward, we increased our pace, our accuracy, and quickly were doing the operations at "Ranger speed" (fast paced and with purpose).

When I work with staffs of sports teams and professional business leaders, I always listen to the choice of words they use. In the sports world and the military, you'll hear "hurry the fu#k up" or "get your head out of your ass" types of statements. We've unfortunately accepted these speech patterns in these professions. Today this type of language has also crept into high school and youth sports, with coaches cursing tirades on young athletes. Then leaders in the business world are talking to their people with the same disdain and negative connotations. We all have heard of Steve Jobs' tirades, and yes, he was extremely successful, but it doesn't make it right.

It's not a rite of passage as a leader to bully or curse someone out. You don't have to do it, and if you're an up and coming leader, don't ever feel like you need to speak that way to prove your worth. If you're selected as a coach or a leader, then coach and lead! Trust me; you will be positively remembered for those you assist in their success and negatively remembered for those you've made to feel less than! Cursing does not equal toughness!

"I've learned that people will forget what you said, people will forget what you did, but people will never forget how you made them feel." ~Maya Angelou

Your language, and more importantly, your use of your language, defines who you are as a leader. Now look, we've all thrown around "F-bombs" and sometimes emotions expose the worst in us. However, when you do feel like you will explode, do not direct this curse-laden tirade towards individuals specifically. Believe me, if a coach, supervisor, or even a friend has ever cursed you out, you will never forget it. Likewise, if you ever did the cursing, I hope you at some point gathered yourself and apologized and refrained from such action again. Verbally abusing someone with profanity goes beyond any cultural or civilized action. You can get your point across by looking people in the eye, using facts in your statements, and speaking clearly and calmly to them.

So, continue to work on your delivery, your speech, your words, and how you get those across to people; this is leadership.

The Take-Away

Your language will define you, both in public and in private.
You can get your point across without having to do the table flip.
Your tone is just as important as what you say.

Don't Be a Screamer

This subchapter goes hand-in-hand with using language appropriately. It's not only the words you use; it's the tone you use them in. Leadership is the ability to know when to give a calm assessment and direction, and also make a correction if the need arises. Let me start by saying that there will be times in your leadership days that you will have to yell. If it's something that could lead to imminent injury or the death of someone, you best be screaming if you need the situation to stop.

Now, I am naturally loud. I have a loud voice and had to do some yelling in my days as both a military leader and a Drill Instructor. I never thought of myself as a constant screamer though, and as my career progressed, I've done less and less of that. Yelling and screaming are only useful when it immediately stops an action that could cost life, limb, or eyesight.

Sometimes raising your voice and giving clear direction can be considered yelling, but if done in a controlled tone, it can be useful. Example, *"Listen up team, when we leave this gate, all eyes will be on us. We must do it right, despite the odds, this is our duty!"* I would say this from time to time in the military when I needed the focus of the Soldiers to understand the importance. Did I yell? No. Was I firm and focused? Absolutely!

I met a business executive on a recent flight, and he was telling me that his boss is nicknamed "Tornado." He said he's an easy going, very dedicated guy but keeps everything in and then "goes storm crazy" on the entire staff and then everything is in havoc for the next 72 hours. In this leader's mind, his thought to keep his team's focus was by holding everything in and then blowing up, screaming at the group! What he was doing is forging a foundation where his team walked on eggshells and would not give honest and timely feed-back for fear that a piece of information would set the boss off!

In 1994, 1st Ranger Battalion and other members of US Special Operations were temporarily stationed on the USS America as the strike platform for operations into Haiti (Operation: Uphold Democracy). As you can imagine, a large unit of Army guys on a Navy Aircraft Carrier posed its own set of challenges. The early days weren't bad as we were preparing and doing our final checks for the very likely event of going into Haiti. The planning was complete, the teams were trained, final briefs conducted, and the mission "GO" order was given. We headed up the lift (commonly used to move the jet fighters from the hanger deck to the flight deck) to our awaiting Black Hawk helicopters, rotors already turning and door gunners loading the mini-guns. It was here, combat mission day and our Ranger Platoon was ready! As we begin to load the aircraft, I see our Platoon Leader, Andy Ulrich, give me the knife hand signal across his throat, signaling mission aborted. I knew this couldn't be good, and when we finally returned to the hanger deck, the word came out as "mission delayed 24 hours."

The 24 hours turned into 40+ days, and now the routine was getting old, and the troops either wanted to go to war and fight or go home. Frankly, I couldn't blame them, but this wasn't my call, and we were facing the undesirable part known as the "boredom of war." Our small platoon bay, which was normally for about 15 occupants, had 32+ Army Rangers shoved in there, gear and all. There was one TV mounted on the wall, and one of our squad leaders, Lee Schmid, rigged up the ship's speaker system in our bay to the TV so everyone could hear it. (Needless to say, the Navy wasn't too happy!) I came back from our daily briefing with our Platoon Leader, and when I entered, there was some Soldier "clowning around" going on.

The boys were frustrated and acting like a bunch of undisciplined teenagers. I knew the frustration had been mounting in me as well. I blew up and began yelling and screaming at the men. Then I went on to scream at a young Ranger who was just inside the doorway and caught in my firing line. I bit this kid's ear off on one side and then the other (figuratively speaking). I was yelling, screaming, and though the men needed it, I went overboard, and this young man took the brunt of my frustration and anger.

I think about this particular day now and then and can still vividly play it over and over in my mind. I lost my composure, and although it was just words, that young man did not deserve the verbal beating. Reflecting on this for many years, and now being older and wiser, I simply should have taken the entire platoon to the flight deck for some lengthy calisthenics. I wouldn't have needed to yell, all the frustrations would have gotten out, and my point would have definitely gotten across without any personal attacks. I never enjoyed verbal blows; they do nothing for me except lessen my motivation or piss me off. Though I've had to comply with those kinds of leaders in the past, I never performed the best under that type of leadership. Go ahead, yell at me, I'll get it done, but I'll never be celebrated under the direction of a screamer. My parents never screamed at me, and my first squad leader in the Rangers, SSG Roberts, never screamed at me. So, I had a foundation forged at a young age.

Let's not misinterpret being tough and getting on someone to get the best out of them as screaming. This happened to me throughout my career, and I did it as well as a leader. However, screaming to scream or prove a point does little except to erode your positive leadership attributes.

Note: The young Ranger I mention in this chapter had a very successful term in the military, then went on to college, and now is a very prosperous businessman, owner, and author. We recently spoke about this incident as it's bothered me for years, and I finally had the opportunity to apologize.

Keeping Your Fingers on the Pulse

Leadership is about giving your subordinates the room to do their job, the ability to think through decisions, and understanding there is no such thing as a zero-defect environment. There are clear lines that may not be crossed and things you cannot do like lie, cheat, or steal, for example.

I had the pleasure of spending a few days with a retired Green Beret Sergeant Major friend. We were enjoying a few German beverages and talking leadership. He is a hero and spent the bulk of his 25-year military career in Special Forces. He will be the first to tell you he learned everything the hard way, and though he achieved the highest Non-Commissioned Officer rank in the U.S. military, his early years were spent gaining and losing the rank of Private. He had good leaders looking out for him. I've found him to be one of the most admirable military leaders of our modern time with a gruff and tough exterior that can frighten the most chiseled warrior! He looked out for Soldiers, counseled them as needed, and always backed them regardless of personality differences. He knew leadership is not a popularity contest, and he wanted men that were accountable, capable, and audacious. They were Green Berets; they had to be great at everything!

As we talked about our careers and shared stories of how we assisted Soldiers in developing their jobs and being successful, he said he would always tell his troops there were two areas in which he would never help them: if they stole money or ammunition. He would counsel Soldiers and advise them that if they violated either one of those rules their career, at a minimum, would be over. Storied and distinguished careers would mean nothing in these cases; he would not be able to advocate for them. A wartime hero's accolades would be over-shadowed because rules were violated. He stressed that when dealing with warriors who are often working in small teams or even alone on assignments, it's important to keep your fingers on the pulse. However, you must do it in a way that allows your talented people to do their jobs.

He had small teams deployed to all parts of Afghanistan doing difficult work in the war on terror. Green Berets are obligated with much more than fighting the enemy; it's nation-building, training indigenous forces, educating the population, safety, security, medical, and everything in between. My friend would travel from camp to camp checking on his brave men and women, making sure if they needed assistance, they received it, but also mentoring and coaching, and keeping his finger on the pulse of what was happening. The travel was exhausting, and between planning and approving combat missions, he barely had time to rest. Yet, he knew this was important to understanding the stress, physical and mental exertion, and tempo of combat operations on his Green Berets.

Keeping your fingers on the pulse and micro-managing are two different animals and not to be confused. If you are managing other people's daily activities and their time, then you are micro-managing. This is not a preferred method of leadership and should only be done in extreme cases such as trying to gain control of a dysfunctional or inexperienced team. You keep your finger on the pulse by asking questions, receiving input, and requiring your team to continue to plan at their current capacity and beyond. Then, and most importantly, you supervise and inspect, get on the ground and walk around and ask more questions. Finally, be observant. Look, listen, and see what's happening throughout the organization. You must become an exceptional listener! Being a "good" listener is not enough in today's leadership arenas.

Consistently change the angle at which you look at things. You can't see what's going on if you look at it through your office window, you must get out of your office and move around. I suggested to a production manager of a company I was doing leadership development for to look at the factory floor from a different angle. I proposed the next time the maintenance team was on a scissor lift doing work, to get on it and look at the process from above. I guaranteed he would see something he would not have seen from the ground level. He called me a few weeks later, having done what I suggested and said, "I couldn't believe how different the process looked and how much I learned!"

I spoke earlier about Colonel Mike Anderson. Besides being a great listener; his observation skills for keeping his fingers on the pulse was at the rock-star level. He was old-school Army, enjoyed his martini after dinner in his quarters, and he smoked a pack a day. He would stand outside at various vantage points at our headquarters several times a day and smoke cigarettes. To the casual observer, he was doing nothing more than taking a "smoke break," however, I quickly noticed he was watching everything happening in the Academy area, and he was keeping his fingers on the pulse.

One day I was in my office filling out the duty roster for the weekend when a newly promoted Army Lieutenant walked in asking if I had seen the Colonel. Knowing he hadn't left for the day, I said to the Lieutenant, "The Colonel is most likely outside his office." The young Officer, physically fit, highly motivated, and not meaning any disrespect said, "Oh, is the old man on a smoke break again?" I smiled and offered him some First Sergeant advice by saying, "Sir, if you think that's all the Colonel is doing…(PAUSE)…then you're not paying attention."

Colonel Anderson knew everything that was happening in our Academy, and you could certainly tell from the questions he would ask the senior staff. He would say things like, "Tell me about the decrease in academic performance in a particular class or subject." Alternatively, he would ask, "Why is Cadet Candidate Smith thinking of leaving the program?" A look of bewilderment would come across the staff, as he would ask precise, very poignant questions. Colonel Anderson was always paying attention and had his fingers on the pulse. One thing synonymous about the wonderful military academies in our country is that they are filled with the best and brightest people working there. Colonel Anderson was clearly the smartest person in the room, but he wouldn't let it show and was never arrogant, rather he wanted everyone's talent to be a part of the success.

The Take-Away

Lead, don't micro-manage.
Keep your fingers on the pulse by asking questions, observing, and "walking the ground," so you know what's happening.
Interact with people at all levels. Whenever possible, you should talk to as many of the people you lead EVERY DAY!

GROUP DYNAMICS AND TEAM CHEMISTRY

Dynamics and chemistry are not a "myth" in leadership; they are a part of the process. You can read leadership book after leadership book, and in at least one of the chapters, you will hear terms like "team dynamics," "building the right chemistry" or "culture," and how these push an organization to success. In business, sports, or life, dynamics and chemistry can be the difference between success and failure.

I'm often asked if a team or a company can be successful if they have poor culture, meager group dynamics, and bad team chemistry. The answer is yes; IF you have an amazing product or your team is filled with the most talented people. Businesses have done well because their product was revolutionary and captured a market. Sports teams have won because they've literally had the best athletes. HOWEVER, this model cannot be sustained, and history has proven this to be correct in both scenarios. If you want to have consistent excellence, to be known as one of the Elite in your particular field, then your culture, dynamics, and chemistry have to be healthy and positive.

In business, and with your team, positive chemistry

can move your team into a position for great success, while bad or negative chemistry can destroy an organization. The chemistry starts with having people of character who are talented. It would benefit workplace cultures if we reward character, embrace it, and use it to assist others in their path for success. By rewarding talent first, you are building an organization that is focused on the winning "highlight" moment that encourages a mindset for instant gratification, which is not sustainable over the long-term. We are very familiar and comfortable with this scenario because it highlights the "plays of the day" and rewards a single significant event. People then work to these individual events and lose focus on their "body of work."

The gap between average and elite is very small. It's often mistaken as such an enormous gap when, in fact, it isn't. If you want to be elite personally or professionally, it takes only a few key attributes. First, it requires you to have sustainable performance. You must be able to do whatever you do very well for a long period of time. There have been companies, teams, entrepreneurs, and athletes who have been what's called a "flash in the pan." Extremely good for a short period of time, but not sustainable. Yes, you can leave a mark (set a record), but you'll never be considered elite.

Next, you must be adaptable at every level. If you do not change with the times and continue to get better, then you will fall behind and eventually be out of business or out of a job. Look at the companies that continued to advance and adapt, Microsoft for example, and those that didn't such as Blockbuster, Kodak,

Yahoo, and JC Penny. The list on both sides is many, and most times, it goes back to a failure to adapt to the changing market and the way people see the world. (Blockbuster, for example, had a chance to purchase Netflix (twice) for a fraction of the price, but didn't see its value.)

Finally, though you need to adapt, improvise, and change, you must stay committed to the process. It will get hard, it's supposed to be hard, and this is when you need to dig in and get it done. Frequently the goal line is just ahead, and generally, it's the last 10 yards that are the most difficult. When it becomes the toughest, victory is just around the corner. Keep going! The teams and organizations who can do this become elite.

How do we get our team to this level? How do we forge a foundation of team chemistry? It starts with "standards." Think of the standards as rules you might have in your own home, for example, shoes off at the front door; lights off in rooms not occupied; cleaning up the kitchen after cooking a meal; locking up the house when you leave; etcetera. You set and maintain standards of excellence that are carried out both as individuals and groups. The same must be done in our places of work in order to build a positive culture. In my days in the Ranger Regiment, we had a "Blue Book" or standards book that went above and beyond Army policies. It covered nearly everything, including such things as how we should dress in civilian clothes, actions to be taken when greeting an Officer, and even how to get our hair cut and how often.

Then it comes down to forming bonds at the lowest

levels. Yes, I said the lowest levels. Often, we want to shove team chemistry down our teams' throats. You will not be a success if you use this method. It's the responsibility of those in the group to get along. I'm not saying it's necessary to sit in a big circle and sing songs, but it is necessary to form working relationships with individuals. These relationships stretch to other individuals, and this is how chemistry is built.

It is your responsibility at the leader level to manage this team chemistry and push or pull it as necessary to ensure it is positive, healthy and meeting the desired ambitions and effectiveness. Team chemistry, if not monitored, can become dysfunctional and lead to disciplinary actions, as well as a failure of goals (remember the finger on the pulse). Subordinates should never control the situation; leaders must always control the group. Leaders do this by setting standards, enforcing those standards, rewarding those who are exceeding the standards, and working with those who are not meeting their potential. This, at times, requires you to discipline and even let people go, but it should only be done after you have exhausted all methods to retrain.

Controlling subordinates is not forcing, threatening, or micro-managing. Being a leader and building team chemistry can be a grueling job; however, education and experience make this a rewarding responsibility. Once you have chemistry in the desired culture, you continue to promote it, stretch it, adapt it to the generational gap, and continue to improve.

If it were easy, then everyone would do it. It requires you to consistently and comprehensively communicate with your team. If a process in the organization needs to change, your people will let you know; however, you must be willing to listen, and always ask them to bring you three courses of action to remedy the problem. Complaining about a problem is easy; finding viable solutions is the most difficult. By developing team chemistry, you will discover that your team will find these solutions, and more importantly, head off issues before they become a problem.

People want to work in an environment where they feel invested, both emotionally and collectively. They want to know that their work and effort is recognized and that their voice is, at a minimum, heard. Everyone has a boss, and sometimes instructions are prescriptive, and you must follow the directive. Nevertheless, when you have a team who is willing to work for each other, even the less desirable tasks will get done correctly and produce results. Tell the entire team what the standard is and work on those few who you know will help you find success. One by one, you begin getting the people of character on board, and then the others will follow. The stubborn ones who are averse to change will self-select out, or become the distractor you will have to discipline and possibly release. Though you want to get everyone moving in the same direction, you will at times have one or two who will just resist. Then you must decide if their talent and skill are worth them being a leadership distractor. I will tell you that eventually, their ability will wear out, and if they are not team-oriented, their usefulness will quickly diminish.

Giving Feedback

Giving feedback as a leader is probably one of the most challenging responsibilities though it sounds very simple. Tell a person what they've done wrong or need to fix, give them a path forward, and move on. A simple process if we were all machines and didn't have the common denominators of "feelings and emotions." None of us wants to be told we've made a mistake, which in the military was referred to as a "soup sandwich." I remember an Army squad leader explaining to a group of Soldiers how a soup sandwich was made, semi-jokingly of course. He said, "You start with a fresh hoagie roll. You split the roll open, and then open a can of chicken noodle soup. You take the soup and pour it onto the hoagie roll, close it up and there you have it, a soup sandwich," or as he eloquently added a "chicken noodle hoagie." Though this is rather funny, no one wants to hear, they are a "soup sandwich."

90% of your message will be in your delivery and the remaining 10% in the content. I can recall asking an

Officer Candidate about his "butt chewing" from a military leader. "What did the Tactical Officer say?" He replied, "I have no idea, he just yelled at me the entire time, and I don't remember a word." At that point, I went in and had a conversation with the Tactical Officer and asked him to clarify what he wanted the young man to know from the feedback session, which he did, and very eloquently as a matter of fact. I took this information and gave the Officer Candidate his areas to improve and a path moving forward. The bottom line: the Tactical Officer had excellent and timely information to help this young man, but his delivery immediately put the Candidate in "shut down mode."

We need to caution the sender in delivering a too overly critical message. As the receiver, you need to listen to the report and extrapolate the keys necessary to move forward. Now I have not always done this right, and you've read about some of my mistakes already. I continue to learn and grow and challenge myself constantly to ensure the message I want to send is getting across correctly. This leads me to my next point: the "opinion."

We all have opinions but remember this; they are ALL subjective. Many times opinions are nothing more than emotions with your "interpretation" of the facts. Views may have interpretations, but facts are different in that they are verifiable. If an opinion is supported by facts, then this becomes an argument. Why did I say all this? I think it's extremely important, especially when you are trying to give feedback, that you state the facts, and keep your opinions to yourself. We want to give people our ideas because many times it's done in good faith. We base our views from previous experiences and want those we are counseling to have as much information as possible. Many times this backfires, and all the person remembers is the "opinion" and fails to look at the facts you have presented.

I can recall doing a leadership seminar for a very successful company and providing them a report on their organization based on a team building exercise and leadership seminar. I gathered all the data from our consultants who were with me at this event and categorized what the company was doing well and the areas to improve. I generally provide this report in person so I can accurately present the findings as sometimes the words written may be misinterpreted. Because of their busy business schedules, it took me a long time to finally get face-to-face with the company leadership.

Most consultants would have tried two or three times and after that just e-mailed the report (we had already been paid for the event). To keep this as simple as possible, the longer it took me to present the report, the more I went over it and the more opinion I put into it. Though it was loaded with factual data from the event, one key and rather glaring opinion was the only thing that stood out. Everything else in the document that held many successes and spoke on areas to improve was now mute. I learned a powerful lesson that day; understanding the focus needs to be on the facts, not on needless opinions.

I did several seminars for the auto industry, and overall, the response was very positive, and everyone took a lot out of it. Several weeks later, the CFO of the company, whom I respect and value her opinion very much, gave us some candid and professional feedback. She had high praise for me and my delivery, and she personally enjoyed it. However, she made a point that it could have been "more descriptive towards their industry" and was "maybe slightly too intense for some in the group." I was thrilled by her assessment as this immediately made me be more self-aware!

Giving feedback can be as easy as the Oreo cookie method. Start off by telling the person what they are doing well, then interject with what specifically they need to work on, and end with either adding something else they are doing well or regurgitating the opening good. There you have it, the Oreo cookie method; Good – Bad (what to improve on) – Good.

Let's not confuse counseling (providing feedback) with mentoring either. When you mentor, you often offer direction based on your experiences and try to guide those under your charge in a positive direction. You must also be mindful when mentoring not to guide the person down "your" path; instead, let them discover what works for them and support them on this quest. The bottom line is that the road should be laid with bricks of success.

The Take-Away

Give feedback using honest and factual data.

Your delivery is key. The fluctuation in your voice can be used more effectively than screaming or yelling.

Beware of using too many opinions, as this can muddy the water. Make your point, be specific, and let that be the lasting memory.

The Power of the Handwritten Thank You

Our world has changed with the power of the computer, smartphones, and social media. We can get information out to many people in a few short keystrokes, and there is much good that has come from that.

When I first became a young Sergeant in the Ranger Regiment (my first time having a team to lead), my father reminded me to say "thank you" to those who have assisted in your career and to those whom you lead. He said, "Thank you works both up and down."

Growing up, I noticed my father would always write people handwritten notes. Sure, he was "old school" as they say, and was never big into the computer information age, although he actually passed his first college computer class at age 88. He reminded me throughout my career that there "was a power in the handwritten note."

I didn't catch on early in my career, but over the last twenty years, I became well-versed in writing small notes of encouragement and saying thank you to those who have made a difference. These notes don't have to be long, just a few lines to tell them their contributions were appreciated and made a difference. I continue to write clients and friends notes, some on WWII pictured note cards or my own personal stationery with meaningful quotes on the back. A handwritten note goes a long way into the "power of people."

I still to this day have a handwritten note on a 1st Ranger Battalion note card from Colonel Pentecost thanking me and telling me I did a great job as a jumpmaster on a particular airborne operation in 1993.

While deployed to Afghanistan in 2008, I received six letters (and still have them) from Colonel Keirsey on unique Civil War note cards, telling me to "stay strong, take care of your Soldiers, and press the fight to the enemy." Colonel Keirsey is an extremely busy man, working, doing professional leadership seminars and technical advisement literally all over the world, yet he "made" the time to write me a few sentences and check on my morale.

I was on a return trip from a leadership session for a major pharmaceutical company a few years ago, and I was able to stop and see one of the leaders who initially hired us to do work. While we were chatting in her office, I noticed next to her family pictures and work documents was a distinctive WWII pictured note card, the one I sent her as a thank you six months earlier. I was honored that she still had it, and it made me appreciate the words my father spoke earlier in my life about the power of handwriting notes.

E-mail, text, social media, etcetera, they are all great. However, if you want to thank someone, then jot down a few sentences on a note card outlining your thanks for their excellent job. It shows the receiver that your words are sincere, and you will be surprised how good it makes you, the sender, feel as well. It takes a little more effort, but it's truly a "win-win!"

The Take-Away

There is always a positive in a handwritten thank you!
These handwritten cards go a long way to inspiring others and leave a positive mark as a leader.
Everyone loves opening mail; give them another reason to smile.

Random Acts of Kindness

It was early spring, 1985 and I was a Private in the U.S. Army assigned to the elite 3rd Platoon, Bravo Company, 2nd Battalion, 75th Ranger Regiment in Fort Lewis, Washington. We had a great platoon loaded with talented individuals and even a few who had cut their teeth on the recent Combat Parachute Assault into Grenada (October 1983) to rescue American college students. The life of a Ranger is a difficult one, both physically and mentally. Every day is a test; every day is a new challenge; every day, you have to show why you are one of our military's most excellent fighting units.

We had a rare weekend off after a very successful week of airborne operations and military training in the field. Our barracks were relatively quiet on the weekends, which I enjoyed. The Rangers who had families or lived off-base were enjoying their time away, and most of the men who lived in the barracks were trying to find reasons to get away and relax. For me, it was the simple things like being able to wash my clothes and prepare my gear for another long week and enjoy a few movies in the room in relative peace.

I walked from my room (which I shared with another young Ranger) to the laundry room and arrived at a place that had two washers and two dryers to service over 30 Rangers. You can do the math and see that this usually doesn't work well. The room was in disarray and packed with military olive-drab laundry bags with dirty, wet and dry clothes thrown in them all over the place. It was your responsibility to do your laundry. The rule was that if you didn't "watch" your laundry, someone could bump you, which meant multiple bags were sopping wet with clothes tossed aside. The place was a mess and not the standard for a Ranger barracks.

For the next several hours I washed, dried and neatly folded the laundry for about seven or eight Rangers who were out doing more important things on the weekend (and I don't blame them!). I finished my laundry as well and left all the other laundry neatly lined up on the drying table and separated by the load. Some bags I knew whom they belonged to by their nametags and some others I had no idea. It didn't matter to me, it was the right thing to do, and frankly, it didn't bother me. It was how I spent this particular Saturday.

Sunday morning, I got up about 0730 (which is considered sleeping in from our regular 0515 wake-ups) and hit the gym with my roommate. We then showered, changed into civvies (civilian clothes) and headed straight for the Ranger Dining Facility (fancy name for mess hall) for Sunday brunch. (The Ranger Dining Facility was known throughout the base to have the best food, the largest portions, and highest quality possible!) Brunch was the best meal of the week, and you could load up on food, and for the most part, no one was going to inconvenience you. It was Sunday; everyone took a break! We finished our meal and were now looking forward to the Sunday afternoon nap! All my gear was ready for next week, my clothes were washed, and I was eagerly anticipating a few hours of relaxation. I had just nodded off, and I hear, "Ranger Spisso, front and center!" I was like, *huh? Did a Sergeant call my name? Moreover, please tell me it wasn't Sergeant MacCarthy!"*

Sergeant MacCarthy was already a combat veteran in the Rangers, having conducted the combat parachute assault into the island of Grenada as a machine gunner. "Sergeant Mac" as he was known wasn't a big man, but he was as reliable as a fireplug and had the brash and bravado to back it up. He was a fitness machine, tough as nails, could battle opponents twice his size and win, and looked as good in civilian clothes as he did in uniform. As Ranger Privates you stayed away from Sergeant Mac because he would quiz you on Ranger history or a weapons system and you could end up doing hundreds of push-ups. He was a tactician and knew his craft.

I hear it again, "Spisso, front and center! I'm not going

to call you again!" My roommate looks at me and says, "JB, you better go before he comes down here and strangles us both!" Good idea! I didn't want to get strangled! I yell out, "Moving Sergeant!" and go tearing out of my room and down the hallway. I stop at the intersection of our platoon entryway a few feet from Sergeant Mac and assume the position of "Parade Rest," the proper position when speaking to a Sergeant. I respond with, "Ranger Spisso, as ordered, Sergeant." (At this point I haven't a clue about why he wants me and was going through in my mind everything in my weekend that I possibly could have screwed up.)

Sergeant Mac says, "Spisso, were you the one that did everyone's laundry this weekend?" I replied, "Yes, Sergeant." He then says, "Did you know my laundry was a part of that?" I replied, "No, Sergeant." He goes on and asks, "So why would you do everyone's laundry and not just leave it there?" I replied, "Seemed like the right thing to do Sergeant, and I didn't mind."

Then, like in the Christmas cartoon *"The Grinch,"* I see a little smile come across Sergeant Mac's face which I've never seen before. He responds with, "Random act of kindness, I'll be dammed! Good job, Spisso, and thank you." I wasn't sure how to respond and felt awkward thanking him back for thanking me, so I made the best response for an 18-year-old Airborne Ranger and just said, "Hooah Sergeant!" ("Hooah" pronounced WHO-AHH is the Ranger universal word that can mean nearly anything but usually connotes "I understand.") Sergeant Mac then says, "I'll see you at morning formation tomorrow Spisso, go enjoy your day. Move out!"

I arrived back at my room; my roommate surprised I'm still alive, and I hit the rack for my Sunday afternoon nap knowing my random act of kindness made a difference on even the most hardened warrior!

The Take-Away

It costs nothing to be kind and helpful, and it fuels your positive spirit.
Kindness is different than being "nice." Kindness is doing something and expecting nothing in return.
Who doesn't like Sunday afternoon naps?

TRANSFORMATION

I call this chapter transformation, but really, it's about the journey to a better you. When I look back at over three decades of learning, leading, and teaching, I see I am in a far better place than when I first got off that bus at Fort Benning, Georgia in 1984. It's not to imply that I didn't have my act together, or I wasn't smart enough, in fact, I was a great teenager growing up and never was in trouble. I studied in school. I was always respectful; however, the journey of learning to lead was just beginning. This is a journey that happens over time. Regardless of your age, if you feel like your leadership is still lacking, you can learn it.

I'm going to emphasize a few things that are common sense but are not always common practice. You need to run your own race. Don't compare yourself to anyone and especially not to somebody on social media. Though there are a lot of great things about these sites, there are just as many that erode your spirit and capitalize on what you think you're failing at, or that you're average, or you're not talented enough. This is all malarkey. You are a masterpiece in your own right! Keep your vision and your focus in front of you and live content in knowing that if you show up every day, put in good work, and don't complain, that you are building success. When you hone your craft in the less visible places, you are fostering the foundation, adding the right mix of sand, gravel, water, and cement. Sometimes (most times) this takes years of work, and then in an instant, the strong footing is built, and then the construction of the framework can continue. When you're working on yourself, your skill set, your transformation, you need to take the time to realize what you have. Be proud of your small wins, your value, your own uniqueness that sets you apart. One of the most rewarding times when I was a Drill Instructor was to observe the face of the family seeing their new Army Soldier after 13 weeks of training. Parents and loved ones are crying with joy, seeing the transformation of their child into the profession of arms. I remember a father asking me, "How did you do it?" I would always reply, "I didn't do it, your son always had it in him. I just chipped away the rough edges." You can transform, you can expand your leadership, and you can find ways to be successful. It's not a cliché, the only thing holding you back is you, and I know you have it in you!

I recently watched a young man cleaning the company's office bathrooms and mopping the common areas where clients enter. He's not in custodial; rather he's the company's shipping and receiving manager. It needed to get done, so he did it! He didn't run around and tell somebody or ask why custodial wasn't in today. He grabbed a mop and mop bucket and went to work. He's forging a foundation for his own success, and I predict this young man will be running his own company one day. He didn't tell anyone he was doing it, no reason for pomp and circumstance; he just did a job that needed doing. He is transforming himself! He is leading by example! He is being the best where he's at currently!

Never use phrases like, "I'll be great once I get to that position" or things like that. Be the best wherever you are. You can't skip the process. Climb the ladder as fast as you want, but you cannot miss a rung, for if you do, you will eventually fall.

Finally, program your mind, or if you need to, reprogram it. Your mind is a super-computer, and just as you have muscles in your body, your brain is the most important muscle – exercise it. Guard your own thoughts; keep your thoughts healthy and positive. If something negative comes into your mind, hit the delete button just as you would on your computer keyboard. Your journey to transform is just that, a journey. Stay steady along the path and celebrate your small wins. You can do it! I believe in you!

The Take-Away

Transformation is the journey to the better you.
Hone your craft in private places; work at it, step by step.
Control your thoughts; they are powerful.

Simplify

Some of the toughest things to do in leadership are:

- Realizing there can always be better ways (even if it's not your way) and
- Not letting past adverse events drain your energy and motivation.

I'm a very positive person and lead that way. I'm a problem solver, cheerleader, and love to inspire and motivate. From time to time, I think about past mistakes I have made, whether personal or professional and feel my energy fading. When this happens, the quicker I shake myself from it, the better off I am, and the same goes for you. Anyone who says they haven't done something they regret is a liar, a fool, or both. I've done a lot of great things in my life, most of which I am very proud. I've also done my share of foolhardy things which lacked the personal courage and character that I live my life by. Bottom line, it's in the past, and the sooner you admit your mistakes, show no fear and rebuild, the better off you will be.

Everyone makes mistakes; however, arrogant people make even bigger mistakes! There are probably three or four instances in your lives you can immediately think of and say, "That was just stupid!" By knowing these times and thinking about them just briefly, will assist in driving your resolve never to repeat those actions. We all have character flaws, but building off of those flaws and using the great attributes you already have to forge your foundation will carve your path for success.

What do most of us want out of life? We can name a variety of things from personal to professional to even specific materialistic items. For most of us, it merely comes down to wanting to be a great partner for our spouse, a loving parent to a child, and being able to be counted on by others. Though this sounds simple, it can be a daunting task. Life throws us curve balls every day, and how we adjust to those is what defines us.

Look, there were times in my life where I wasn't a good husband, or father, and just an average leader to those under my charge. My plate was so full I became average at everything! We think by accepting more we can do more, but in reality, we do less. Simplify your life by taking the few things which are indeed important and become great at those. It doesn't happen overnight, and many times you need some assistance doing this.

I'm saying to make the time spent with your spouse, your family, and those under your charge, meaningful. Meaningfulness is not based on time. In fact, if you measure it with time, then your focus is off, and you've already lost. Don't multi-task when someone is talking to you; take a moment to get your head up, put your phone down, look them in the eye, and really listen to what they have to say. Those few minutes of undivided attention will produce long-term dividends.

When Bill Clinton was the President of the United States, I was fortunate to be invited to a White House breakfast on Memorial Day. This was truly a highlight and, though I was already a decorated military and combat veteran at the time, I was in awe of the experience. Towards the end of the breakfast, there was a receiving line where you get to meet the President, as well as other senior government leaders. As I was approaching the President, the first thing I personally noticed was he's taller than I expected. He was greeting everyone kindly and shaking hands and saying hello. Each encounter took about 20-30 seconds. There was a photographer snapping pictures, and somehow you ended up with an 8x10 picture of you and the President. I was thrilled and somewhat nervous. When it was my time to meet President Clinton, he shook my hand and asked me where I was from and how long I had been serving in the Army. Then he began to look over my uniform, as if I were on a formal inspection and began to ask me about my unit patch, what duty position I was currently serving in, and about my experiences at both West Point and in the Rangers. The receiving line came to a dead stop, and when a White House official tried to move me along, the President just looked at him, and he immediately backed away.

For the next five minutes, or so it seemed, the President of the United States had a unique and detailed conversation with me, an enlisted man, about the Army, my training, and my family. His eyes were glued on mine, and he spoke to me as if he had known me his entire life. The busiest person in America (maybe the world), spent five minutes focused, attentive, in conversation with me. Sure, it was only five minutes, but it felt like five hours! It goes back to "undivided attention."

You need to simplify your time too. Take alone time for yourself, 20 minutes a day is all you need. Use this time to gather your thoughts, appreciate life, and focus on the future. A little "appreciating the good stuff" is perfect for the soul. I like to take my 20 minutes first thing in the morning. Sitting at our kitchen island in total quiet enjoying a cup of coffee. I do a little reading from a variety of inspirational books. I have three or four books going at once, and each day I choose one and read just a few pages or even a chapter. It keeps it fresh, and many times, I get a little "boost" for the day. I use this time to get my mind "right," well before I write or review my daily task list or head to the gym. This short focus period gives my mind time to set itself for the day, regardless if it's an arduous one or not. If I'm traveling and have an early AM flight, I take the time on the plane to do the same thing, a few minutes of positive thought before I prepare myself in detail for the day's events. This is called balance; this is called simplifying your life; this is what the best leaders always do!

It's true we need an equal amount of healthy stress and enjoyment to stay in balance. If you have too much of either, then your mind, body, and soul will be out of balance. Simplifying your life by attacking it in small chunks. I like to call this "fighting the small battles." Life painted with a broad stroke can be very challenging and even threatening. Breaking it into small chunks will allow you to accurately accept the challenges and focus on the positives of each task.

When it's time to work out, then work out! I see people in the gym on their phones, talking, texting, or going through their music to find the right song. Get in there, get your workout in, and get out.

When it's time to be at work, then be at work. Jump

in with both feet and face the challenges head-on. Many people ask me if I tackle the toughest challenge first or chip-away at the small ones and leave the biggest to last. You need to find what works for you because one theory doesn't work for all. Personally, I attack the small ones, and once I get a rhythm going, then I tackle the tough one. I like to get a little warmed up! Stay motivated on the tasks, even when they become challenging (especially when they become difficult!).

When it's time to be home or enjoy your kid's soccer game, then do just that. Getting home at 5:00 pm to work another three hours at home while ignoring your family doesn't balance the family portion. You're better off getting home at 6:30 pm if your workload is that full and focusing the next few hours entirely on your family. Balance is the only way you can effectively lead to a consistent amount of time and be able to do it with calm clarity. If your life focus is out of balance, the result is you end up doing nothing well.

When I was going through personal difficulties, my life was out of balance. I had to find ways to focus my energies on the task at hand. It was difficult; I had decisions about finances, children, and business, which all needed my energy and attention. I was fighting in all directions. The old military analogy of "when you try to defend everywhere, you end up defending nowhere" is what happened to me and it took me years to recover on a personal and professional level. What I learned was to focus my energy on the primary mission during that time. If it's eight hours while at work, then put all your energy into that. Table the other distracters and focus on them at their appropriate times. If you have legal matters that need to be addressed, then take two-hours of personal time from work and go and fix those. Staying at your desk and trying to work on your private needs defeats both purposes.

When it's time to focus on your children, then give them your 100% focus and put aside any other distractors. Refresh your mind and get back on track. In these types of complex issues, something will have to be sacrificed, which is usually sleep and personal time. So, I urge you if you have something out of balance, work diligently to get it into balance. Don't ignore it; it won't fix itself. Never forget there are times you will also need to be a survivor! These difficult times will also pass, stay focused, stay the positive course.

The Take-Away

Find the balance in your life between stress and enjoyment.

Balance is critical in making sound and timely decisions while keeping unnecessary emotions in check.

Everything you do in life should keep you on the path for success; if something doesn't, then eliminate it.

Focus

We are in the information technology age, and electronic devices surround us. They are the sources to stay in touch, send and receive information, and allow us the ability to get things done faster. We use them, we count on them, and we can quickly become addicted and dependent on them. It's called information overload, and it can affect your daily life if not controlled. Too much of anything is never a good thing. This subchapter focuses on your mental health and the necessity of taking the time to *FOCUS and SHUT IT OFF!*

In most gym and workout facilities, it usually states, "no cell phone use in the workout area." Though this is posted and even announced over their public address system, you still have plenty of people who make and take calls while working out. Now, this doesn't bother me except for the fact that I know those people aren't focused on their workout; their mind is filled with other priorities. Do they do this when they're home, at work, at their kids' hockey game?

I have about a ten-minute drive to the gym, and I used to make a quick call to a client or friends on the drive there and checked a few emails in the parking lot before going in. What I found was that my mind was not focused as it should be when it was time to get to the workout. I have fixed that issue and either leave my phone at home or shut it off before I leave for the gym. I now use the short drive to relax my mind, and when I get to the gym its "business" for the next 45 minutes to an hour. I don't use this time to chit-chat or spend time at the juice bar. I get in, get fit, and get out. My mind is refreshed, and my body is as well!

I fully understand for most of us our phones are a link to our business, profit margin, and our lives. However, taking the time to focus on different objectives during the day makes you more productive, healthier, and you guessed it, happier!

In working with a particular professional sports team, I noticed when the players showed up for work, they were on their phones, hit the computers in the players' lounge, and seemed pre-occupied instead of focused on their craft. Sure, you need some time to get settled and to get going, but practice time is so precious (and really very short), you have to make every minute count. So, after discussing with the coach, the next day he put all phones and computers off-limits until their practice day was done. If they had issues at home, their significant other would know whom to call. "Get here, get focused, and get it done," is what the coach told them. When they walk into the player's entrance, it is time for business, whether it's practice, video, workouts, or treatments.

This doesn't mean you can't enjoy yourself through-out the day; on the contrary, you should enjoy your work. But, when you're at your "craft," then focus on your craft. It took a few days of adjustment, but the team actually rallied around the "rule," and they were spending more time talking with each other instead of checking social media or booking a tee-time.

Again, when you're at the gym, focus on the gym, when you're with your family, focus on your family. When it's time to be on the phone fielding calls, then field your calls. You will be pleasantly surprised at how much more efficient and capable you are when you take time away from the phones, computers, think pads, and any other sources of communication and information.

You should do this with your children. How many of

you receive texts from your kids while you are both inside your house? They need to shut it off as well and spend some time with face-to-face communication. Draw a picture, write a letter, or pick up an actual magazine!

In conducting a leadership session for a group of Senior Vice Presidents, one of them mentioned that he was always home for dinner by 6 pm every night. My first thought was, *that's great! Here is someone finding a way to sectionalize their life and spend time appropriately on work, as well as with his family.* The truth of the matter was he would come home by 6 pm, have dinner, then spend the next three hours in his home office doing more work. So, though he was "there," he wasn't! Instead, I told him to stay at work if he needed to finish a project or plan his day a little better. He was infamous for having meeting after meeting. I urged him to cut the meetings down to twice daily; a quick update brief in the morning lasting no more than 15 minutes and then a wrap-up meeting later in the day. Use the additional time to complete your work, and when you go home, spend that time as a great father, husband, and role model for your family.

The best leaders have been able to do what I call "sectionalize" parts of their life. Your life is a valuable painting; don't use a paint roller when a fine brush is really what you need. The personal relationships you build with friends and family, taking time to make a difference in someone's life, and understanding that though material and financial success are great, they don't define who you are; this is leadership, this is the focus.

The best realize that to maintain their effectiveness, they need to build that valuable recovery wave by doing other things besides just work. Alone time is an essential ingredient in our healthy lifestyle. Whether it's time away at the spa or sitting on the couch watching your favorite sporting event in total peace, it is necessary for your mental health. Laughter is also a way of building that wave, especially being able to laugh at yourself from time to time. If you can't be confident enough to laugh at yourself once in a while, leading will get both boring and challenging.

Preparing yourself for bed is just as important as making yourself ready for the workday. About an hour before you want to go to sleep, make a list of the things you need to do for the next day and start winding your mind down by turning off all electronics, including the TV. Pick up something easy or inspirational to read. This is known as "sleep hygiene," and it is proven to work.

Take time to thank and hug your families and those close to you, spend quality time with them, and savor the process of life. Enjoy. Hooah!

The Take-Away

Fight the "small wars;" don't paint your life with broad strokes.

You will survive if your phone is shut off from time to time; trust me! You might even like the time away.

Prepare yourself with "sleep hygiene" before bed.

> Your brain needs rest as much as your body does.

Be Happy in Others' Success

I was attending a graduation many years ago and while sitting in the auditorium with hundreds of other parents and family members, I was listening to all the chatter about who was graduating where (in what number position), who was going to what particular college, and which graduates didn't get in to the colleges they were hoping to get into. I always shy away from gossip, as it is an unnecessary drain on your energy, but I was getting a little laugh listening to everyone.

A young man was being presented as the Valedictorian and came up to give his speech, which was rather witty and well done and not the typical "canned" speech you usually hear from the person in this position. The gossip continued from a few people near me, and all I could think was "just be happy for this kid!" He worked his tail off to be in this position and regardless if you think he's the right person or not, he's it; he's giving his speech!

Being happy for other people is something that comes from separating your ego, personal agenda, and regimented beliefs from the situation. Some people have more success than others, that's a fact. Some people are more blessed with talent than others; that's a fact. Some people fall into better opportunities than others; this too, is a fact. However, being pissed-off, jealous, envious, or having self-pity, resentment, or anger towards others does nothing but push you further away from your own goals. Your personal and professional success is forged from what you do. You must not engulf yourself in how others' success is formed. You've heard me say this, before, "run your own race."

Countless people have told me, "I'll help you out with your business" or "give you tips to writing your book." The truth of the matter is, few do come through to help you, and this is a fact of life. However, the ones who do come through to help, actually want you to succeed because they are people happy in the success of others.

There are a lot of people who are in the leadership and culture development business and others who call me for help or advice on their pursuit; I help them. If it's not something I specifically do, I put them in touch with a friend or colleague who may be able to assist them. The point of the matter is there is plenty of success to go around.

I understand that some people find their specific "niche" and don't want anyone to disrupt that for them. These people are content only in their happiness and success, and they measure it in dollars rather than in their commitment to their fellow human. Caring, sharing, assisting, and inspiring others is the foundation of who we are. Be happy for those around you and be positive in your feelings for them. Use the positives to fuel your inner warrior spirit.

Ask yourself these questions:

- What are my talents?
- How can I use those talents to better my life and those around me?

Being happy for others will do more than make them feel good; it will make you feel good and draw positive effects to you in the long run. You've heard the term karma. What you give is generally what you receive in return, so why not give some "good" to others! Success is built over time, with integrity and through a lasting commitment to excellence, both for yourself and others. Stay after your goal, chip away at it, and celebrate the tiny victories. Remember, you don't have to prove anything to anyone else. Show it to yourself!

The Take-Away

You will find more personal success when you are happy for others.
If you have a goal, find your own private "drive" to get it done.
Thank those who have helped you along the way.

Positive Spirit = Victory

Being positive is more than just words; it's a belief and a way of life. It is not to be confused with hope because things will not always get better on their own. However, living with a code of having a positive mental attitude will be a foundation for a beautiful life.

Too often, we measure success in monetary and physical things. I know people who are wealthy beyond belief but are just miserable humans. I quickly disassociate myself with them because I don't want that negativity on me. If you're going to win, if you're going to succeed, then your victory starts with having a positive spirit. Human beings aren't as complicated as we try to make them. Simply, what most humans need are love, faith, and meaningful work. This work can range from a C-suite executive to a homemaker. If it's useful and making a difference, and it's fueled by a positive spirit, it's then rewarding, and that my friends, equates to wins.

A lot of my work is with business and sports teams, and it starts with forging a positive culture. To focus on winning, without the healthy and positive spirit, is running a race backward. It can be done. You might finish the race, but you'll never see or enjoy where you are going. Whatever or whomever your higher power is; religion, family, community, education, etc. . . . start every day with that power. Begin your day with the positive energy to fuel your fire and your success. Don't put a measure on your progress with material things; because a beautiful home without love in it, is just a structure; a house with love is captivating.

One of my good friends and one of the best strength and conditioning trainers out there is a man by the name of Reason Chandler. There is not a client who walks into his facility that isn't pleasantly greeted with a smile, a handshake, and his famous "what's up, what's up, what's up!" It doesn't matter what type of day he is having, or what kind of day you're having, he lifts your spirits and wants you to win, and knows that you cannot get the best workout possible unless your mind and spirit are ready to win. The body will follow along.

I've known people who will backstab, defame, claw, scratch, fight, or use any means possible to win. At the end they might have achieved victory, but what have they done? They used their energy to be negative, to fight negative, and to win negative. Now, for some people, this is all they know because they grew up hard, maybe without parents, broken homes, even homeless, so looking at the world in a positive light is almost impossible. I'm telling you if you look at it differently, stop negatively complaining that you didn't get that break, or accepted into that school, or that promotion, and say "it's all part of a positive experience," then you will begin to use the "positive-fight" mentality. The energy of being positive is not magical, and it's not a gimmick, and there are thousands of books written on this subject alone. The positive spirit will lead you on the right path.

Surround yourself with positive and uplifting people. If you work around the negative types, try to assist them in their affirmative spirit and if they don't want any of it, well then you might have to eat your lunch alone. If you hang around people that give up, then you will give up. If you hang around those who are always gossiping about the boss behind their back, then you will start doing that. Stand up for yourself and be accountable for yourself. Every single moment you think positive and make yourself feel positive you are changing the chemistry in your body for the better. Then it begins to take hold, and it becomes this positive wildfire that uplifts you. Sure, not every day is going to be a day full of puppies and rainbows, but you can always control your positive attitude and your outlook. Give it a try!

How We Grow

Growing, developing, improving, and getting better is
all a part of our life. Regularly we put a schedule to it,
and we plan accordingly to ensure we are meeting our
desired goals, but the speed doesn't matter as long as
you are moving forward.

I was fortunate to graduate from college with little
debt because of the U.S. Army college fund and other
Veteran's programs while I served. Due to an intense
work schedule, I chiseled away at my degree taking one
class at a time, and after nearly 20 years, I received my
Bachelors of Science degree in Organizational Man-
agement from Nyack College. Many times, we gauge
our success by what's happening around us, or to
others, or by pre-determined timetables. If you take
anything from this book, let it be this: be yourself and
keep making positive steps in the right direction!

Growing, just like planting a seed, has its dark period.
Stop looking at the dark as something negative or not
useful; rather it's a stage of preparation where the
crucial work is happening to develop your growth. This
is the time to water the soil, cultivate it, nurture it, add
sunlight and water, and continue to trust and inspire

your mind, body, and soul. If you want to get better at anything, become smarter, faster, stronger, healthier, tougher, etcetera, you need to focus on three simple yet key areas:

- Positive habits
- Routines and repetition
- Having the right recording

The military puts new recruits through the paces early and often during initial entry training. In a matter of a few days, things like fitness, marching, and Soldier skills are becoming a part of their mental and physical memory banks. They do this by ensuring it happens every day, at nearly the same time, and the mind and body become accustomed to the initial stress. As the days move on, the stress goes down, and you may continue to add additional training (stressors) into place. This is the same for you! If you want to accomplish your goals and dreams, then you need to put a disciplined, timely, and encouragingly focused agenda into action.

Positive habits are nothing more than something you're doing that produces a constructive benefit or action. If you want to wake up well-rested, then you need to get an appropriate amount of sleep every night, for example. The positive habit would be to get to sleep at the desired time, so you have the full sleep term (generally this is 8 hours for best results).

Routines and repetitions are actions on your program and adding frequency to them. For example, you go to the gym four times a week. You add this to the positive habit by ensuring it's in your schedule, you're actually doing it, and putting in the effort of the sequence, so you reach your fitness goals.

You must play the right recording for yourself. This is just as important, if not more so than the others. What are you saying to yourself? How are you saying it? I'm fortunate to work with executives and athletes. In some cases, they are the toughest critics on themselves. (I think we all are in some situations at least.) I remind them of the success they have achieved and to always speak in a "positive spirit and tone."

What you speak, you receive. Speak positivity, glory and favor, and you will receive these. The brain is a powerful muscle, and just as you physically train your body, you can do so with your brain. Each of us has a purpose, and we are all professionals at something. Never speak defeat or lack, rather speak the positivity that we all hold within us. Accentuate what you're good at, your talents, your gifts, and those tools you were born with and developed and set you apart from everyone else.

Finally, sometimes our hopes and dreams can be shattered by the jealousy of others or even our family who feels we're not talented enough. This is all nonsense. Find those one or two people who you trust, and if they are truly in your corner, they will inspire you to follow the path and be sincerely happy for you when success flows your way. It only takes one person to believe in you or give you a shot, someone who makes a call or recommendation that opens a door. In the end, you don't have to prove it to anyone else, not a coach, a co-worker, former boss, or even a relative. All you need to do is prove it to yourself! Your positive self-worth, your right recording, it all starts with you!

The Take-Away

Positive spirit isn't magic, or a gimmick, it's a true belief and can be mastered.
Put your schedule together, get on it, and do it.
Positive habits can be built and sustained in just weeks!

WARRIOR LEADERSHIP: ENJOY THE JOURNEY

You're at the finish line, and now it's time for you to take responsibility for your own growth. In this final chapter, I want to leave you with some thoughts for your personal "call to action." I will highlight a few of the key points, and you may consider this chapter as your all-encompassing take-away.

This is your race, you own it, only you can run it, and you must take responsibility for it. Whether life dealt you a great hand or you're holding the worst cards at the poker table, it's your responsibility to play the cards you've been dealt. You control You! Your attitude and effort define who you are and tell a lot of who and what you can become. If you have a head start in life, great; and if you don't, it doesn't mean you can't be just as successful, or more!

Life is full of two key components, talent and grit. Talent you are born with, but grit is the key that pushes your talent to be its best! Sharpen your skills by learning as much as you can; there is so much information available to you today that "not knowing" is nearly irrelevant.

Invest in your health and welfare. If you can't afford

a gym membership, there are hundreds of free online workouts. Workout in your apartment, or, better yet, get outside (this is the best actually). Be strategic in your development, and take steps to grow. Sharpen your ax, as they say. Work on those small skills, so when it's time to face the giant, you're prepared and ready!

Everyone knows the Biblical story of David and Goliath, and I do believe there was involvement from a higher power (God). However, while David was doing what many thought (including his family) was a meaningless job tending to sheep in the field, David was perfecting his skills with the slingshot. He could hit a target 100-yards away, and if a predator were coming close to the sheep, he would nail them with a rock flung from his slingshot. David practiced and practiced in the "dark places." When it was time to face Goliath, he did so with ease because he was prepared: mentally, physically, spiritually, and emotionally.

Find a mentor, someone better and more successful than you. Take this person for coffee or a smoothie, or meet them at the gym. Ask a few meaningful questions, then listen and learn. Develop your talents and don't get destination disease. If you're comfortable where you are, you're not challenging yourself; you need to keep climbing. Maybe you've reached your own level of success. Then help others reach theirs! You should write a personal growth plan and update it every 3 to 5 years. List what your next steps are (research those steps), challenge those around you to push you further, and you do the same for them.

While you're grooming your talents and waiting for the next big break, improve right where you are. Be a superstar in what you're doing right now, in the role asked of you! It's amazing how many personal development classes you can take online for little to sometimes no money. I'll say it again, learn and grow!

A vital quality of being a great leader is having good manners. When I see a senior executive or veteran athlete acting all brash and pompous and speaking down to people, I know this is exactly how they acted when they were younger. Similarly, when I see a seasoned leader getting their own coffee, talking politely to others, holding the door for random people, helping out the "rookie" so others don't ridicule them, I know this is who they have always been, or they learned it. You are expected to have good manners at all levels, keep this reminder as a close learning tool.

There are 86,400 seconds in each day or 1440 minutes. Take 20 minutes each day for your own personal development (reading, learning, studying, improving), 30-45 minutes at some type of fitness activity (even just walking), and 15 minutes with a mentor or mentoring someone else. That's only 80 minutes a day that will solidify your foundation for your development and success. If you do this each day for one year, you will have spent 29,200 minutes improving. There's no way you won't be better! Find your own formula that works for you, experiment, try new things, and develop those countless talents that are held inside of you!

I hope you enjoyed this book; I really enjoyed writing

it and putting it together, and I thank you sincerely for reading it. For more tips on how you can be a Warrior Leader, visit my website at www.jbsleaders.com or email me at info@jbsleaders.com for information.

"If your actions inspire others to dream more, learn more, do more and become more, you are a leader."

~John Quincy Adams

ABOUT THE AUTHOR

JB has over 30 years of experience in transforming individuals into leaders.

He is a veteran of the United States Army with 26 years of service, including ten years in Special Operations with the elite 75th Ranger Regiment, leading the Country's most talented Soldiers in combat. JB retired at the prominent rank of Sergeant Major, the highest and most respected Non-Commissioned Officer position in the military.

JB is extensively well-versed as a leader, trainer, and educator. He has executed effective team building and leadership training for several collegiate and professional sports teams, including NFL and NHL clubs, and was the first in the National Hockey League to hold the position of Executive Director of Leadership and Cultural Development, spawning similar roles with other professional teams throughout the league.

He routinely advises C-Suite executives on leadership and culture and is a sought-after speaker for industry gatherings and leadership podcasts.

With JB, what you see is what you get. He is a motivator with an energetic passion for helping others. He understands the rigors, the risk, the teamwork, and the mindset needed for success.

For more information on scheduling leadership,
culture, and/or team building training,
or to enlist JB as a speaker, please visit:
www.jbsleaders.com
or email JB at
info@jbsleaders.com

WHAT OTHERS ARE SAYING

"I have witnessed JB lead and interact with well-known CEOs and Generals to the lowest ranking Private in Foreign Armies. He has the ability to identify organizational and leadership deficiencies and develop a realistic plan of action to make improvements. His only way to lead is by example."

~William Hart, Captain (Ret), US Army, Sergeant – NYPD

"Everyone needs strong leadership skills to maximize their potential, reach the next level, and bring the team along with them. Great leaders seek mentors like JB to challenge them and their teams to elevate an organization's performance. With his guidance, I have learned to stay the course, dismiss distractions, advance my leadership skills, and prepare for success."

~ Christine Obadal, Managing Partner, Gartner Federal Consulting

"If you want to take your leadership skills to unimaginable heights, there is no better resource than JB o to help you achieve your goals. JB is an artist. He can sculpt anyone who is open-minded and has a desire for personal growth into the kind of leader they dream of being. He is a man of action. I have watched him re-tool a corporation for success and witnessed the positive effect he has on business leaders and athletes; both professional and amateur. He truly cares about people and demonstrates incredible concern for others. JB works at both the group and individual level to help you become the best you can be, and he will equip you with the right attitude to deliver abundant success."

~Richard Parker, CEO/President, Business Owner

"JB has been an exemplary leader, mentor, and coach both in and out of the military. He cares deeply about the success of his mentees and friends and will go out of his way to help them realize their full potential. As a mentor and friend, he is always there to inspire, encourage, and push you through the ups and downs of your career and personal life. When advising a company or a group of executives, he applies long-term thinking and focuses on lasting success of the leaders and organizations. He has been a true inspiration and a role model to numerous athletes, executives, and current and former military personnel both in the U.S. and internationally. I hope, through this book, many more will benefit from JB's unique perspectives and insights which are applicable both professionally and personally."

~John J. Kim, Investment Broker

ACKNOWLEDGMENTS

I want to thank God for my life, my family, and my ability to inspire others.

To my parents, Patricia and John E. Spisso, thank you for laying a firm foundation for me through your kindness, love, and caring. Until we meet again . . . I miss you every minute of every day.

To my sisters, Johnette and Johnese, who have made success in life look easy because they were never afraid of hard work and instilled that in me.

Thank you to Lona Spisso who helped me take my initial monstrous manuscript and cut it down to a readable level, leaving me plenty of material for a second book. Sometimes we can't see the forest for the trees.

To Lieutenant Colonel (Ret.) Hank Keirsey who wrote the Foreword to this book. Thank you for your sage advice. Your guidance allowed me to become a reliable and committed leader, and more importantly, a better man and father.

From my career in the military, I wish to thank each of the warriors who have given me tools for my leadership tackle box. You are so numerous that naming each of you would fill chapters. I am forever indebted! And to all those who have volunteered to serve our Country in some capacity, thank you. Hooah!

To all of those I have been honored to meet outside the military. You too are warriors who have solidified my foundation as a winner and one who cares more about helping others than his own accomplishments. I have learned ten-fold from you than you have learned from me. My sincerest thanks will never scratch the surface of how grateful I am.

Finally, to the Power Family and all those who live in and around me; great people who do great things every day by upholding family values, raising their kids to have Honor and Courage, and the ones I know can be counted on if the red star cluster goes up and we must rally at Freedom Rock.

57873366R00075

Made in the USA
Middletown, DE
02 August 2019

> *"Efforts and courage are not enough*
> *without purpose and direction."*
> *-John F. Kennedy*

JB Spisso's mission is this; to transform individuals into leaders. It's a mission honed with over 26 years of military service, leading in some of the most elite troops and schools in the United States. An interesting thing about the military, every warrior, regardless of rank, is considered a leader. *Warrior Leadership* embodies this philosophy. It doesn't matter if you're a seasoned CEO or a first-time manager, captain of a sports team, or a stay-at-home mom. Each of us has the ability, and, more importantly, the responsibility to lead.

To be a warrior means choosing to put in the hard work to become the best you can be in whatever role you have and to do so with honor, courage, and character. Warriors inspire others to do more and be more. They are a "force multiplier" – the catalyst for significantly increasing an individual's, team's, or organization's potential for success. Warrior leaders constantly transform, learn, and adapt.

Warrior Leadership uses real-life examples to lay out the steps necessary to become the leader you were intended to be. From finding your leadership style to enhancing group dynamics and team chemistry, JB tackles these topics like the warrior he is; talking as much about his failures and what he learned, as his successes. After all, warriors learn from warriors. Are you ready?

ISBN 9781733275804

90000